Linkages of Financial Groups in

Linkages of Financial Groups in the European Union

Financial Conglomeration Developments in the Old and New Member States

by Ingrid Ulst

CEU PRESS

Central European University Press

Budapest   New York

©2005 by Ingrid Ulst

Published in 2005 by

Central European University Press
An imprint of the
Central European University Share Company
Nádor utca 11, H-1051 Budapest, Hungary
Tel: +36-1-327-3138 or 327-3000
Fax: +36-1-327-3183
E-mail: ceupress@ceu.hu
Website: www.ceupress.com

400 West 59th Street, New York NY 10019, USA
Tel: +1-212-547-6932
Fax: +1-646-557-2416
E-mail: mgreenwald@sorosny.org

ISBN 963 7326 12 X   cloth
ISBN 963 7326 11 1   paperback

Library of Congress Cataloging-in-Publication Data

Ulst, Ingrid.
Linkages of financial groups in the European Union : financial conglomeration
developments in the old and new member states / by Ingrid Ulst.-- 1st ed.
   p. cm.
Includes bibliographical references and index.
1. Financial services industry--European Union countries. 2. Conglomerate
corporations--European Union countries. I. Title.

HG186.A2U47 2005
332.1'094--dc22
                   2005007262

Printed in Hungary
by Akadémiai Nyomda, Martonvásár

Table of Contents

List of Tables   vii
List of Graphs   ix

Introduction   1
Chapter 1
Financial Conglomeration: Economic and Legal Aspects   7
1.1. Nature and Features of Financial Conglomeration   7
1.2. Why Financial Conglomeration?   11
   1.2.1. Developments of Conglomeration   11
   1.2.2. Reasons for Conglomeration   16
      1.2.2.1. Motives of Financial Institutions   16
      1.2.2.2. Driving Forces of Conglomeration   23
      1.2.2.3. Economics of Conglomeration   28
1.3. Risks and Safeguards of Financial Conglomeration   31

Chapter 2
Financial Conglomeration in the European Union   41
2.1. Banking in the European Union: Importance and Insurance Linkages
   of Largest Banks   41
2.2. Insurance in the European Union: Importance and Banking Linkages
   of Largest Insurance Undertakings   53
2.3. Major Banking-Insurance Groups in the European Union   59

Chapter 3
**Financial Conglomerates of the European Union in The New Member
States**   69
3.1. Banking and Insurance Sectors in the New Member States   69
3.2. Presence and Importance of the European Union Banking-Insurance
   Groups in the New Member States   72
   3.2.1. Largest Banks in the New Member States and the European
      Union Linkages   73
   3.2.2. Largest Insurance Undertakings in the New Member States and
      the European Union Linkages   79
   3.2.3. Presence of the European Union Banking-Insurance Groups in
      the New Member States   84

3.3. M&A Activities of the European Union Banking-Insurance Groups in
   the New Member States   90
   3.3.1. Banking-Insurance Sector M&A Experience   90
   3.3.2. M&A Criteria: Case Studies   95
3.4. Opportunities and Threats of Financial Conglomeration   102
   3.4.1. From the Perspective of Institutions   104
   3.4.2. From the Perspective of Countries   110

Conclusion   117
Abbreviations   123
References   125
Sources of Research Data   129
   Internet Sources   129
   Databases   132
Index   133

List of Tables

Table 1. Largest Banks and Linked Insurance Undertakings in the EU as of 31 December 2001   42

Table 2. Key Figures of the Largest Banks and Banking Groups as of 31 December 2001   46

Table 3. Largest Banking Sector M&A Deals in the EU   50

Table 4. Largest Insurance Undertakings and Linked Banks in the EU as of 31 December 2001   54

Table 5. Major Banking-Insurance Groups in the EU as of 31 December 2001   62

Table 6. Largest M&A Deals between EU Banks and Insurance Undertakings in 1990-2001   66

Table 7. Structure of Banking and Insurance Sectors in the New Member States as of 31 December 2001   70

Table 8. Largest Banks and Banking Groups in the New Member States as of 31 December 2001   74

Table 9. Largest Insurance Undertakings in the New Member States as of 31 December 2001   80

Table 10. EU Banking-Insurance Groups in the New Member States as of 31 December 2001   85

Table 11. M&A Activities of EU Banking-Insurance Groups in New Member States, 1990–2002   91

Table 12. Erste Bank Results in Central Europe   96

Table 13. FDI Inflows in Central and Eastern Europe (USD Mio)   102

List of Graphs

Graph 1. Total Assets of Five Largest Banks and Banking Groups in the
        EU as of 31 December 2001   47

Graph 2. Market Shares of Five Largest Banks as of 31 December 2001   48

Graph 3. Total Assets of Largest Insurance Undertakings in the EU as of
        31 December 2001   58

Graph 4. Insurance Premiums in the EU and World Market as of
        31 December 2001   59

Graph 5. The Largest Banks and Banking Groups in the New Member
        States as of 31 December 2001   78

Graph 6. The Largest Insurance Undertakings in the New Member States
        as of 31 December 2001   83

Graph 7. EU Country Linkages in the New Member States as of
        31 December 2001   89

Introduction

The most general definition of beauty... Multeity in Unity.
(Samuel Coleridge, On the Principles of Genial Criticism, 1814)

Small is beautiful but also small. In the light of continuous globalisation, all sectors face increasing openness and small is often considered a disadvantage when it comes to increasing competitiveness and profitability of firms. Economies of scale and scope play an important role in major business sectors of the world, the financial sector among them. Is large always and unconditionally the best alternative for firms and economies?

During recent years the financial services industry has faced a drastic worldwide increase in deregulation that has significantly reduced barriers to competition among financial services providers. Continuous improvements in the field of information and communication technology have created "the world without borders" by allowing greater geographic reach via different electronic channels. In the light of recent developments, the financial services industry has followed the similar pattern as other commercial sectors and has shown trends of extensive consolidation. Furthermore, in addition to the local and cross-border consolidation across the same type of financial institutions, financial consolidation has also shown trends of increased consolidation across different types of financial institutions.

Financial conglomeration has created a large number of economies of scale. Financial services providers in the 15 former European Union member states[1] (hereinafter "EU") play an important role both in worldwide financial conglomeration and conglomeration in the European region. This book discusses the promises and pitfalls of financial conglomeration and examines the reasons for M&A activities across different types of financial institutions. The book focuses on banking-insurance

---

[1] The 15 former European Union member states (EU-15) are the states which were members of the European Union before the enlargement on 1 May 2004. Only those 15 member states are taken into consideration whenever the terms "EU" or "the European Union" are used in this book.

conglomerations in the EU and respectively on conglomeration linkages between the EU and its 10 new member states (hereinafter 'new member states').[2] The book addresses the developments of conglomeration between the EU-originated financial conglomerates and the institutions in the new member states. The book also discusses the benefits and risks related to financial conglomeration across borders.

Objectives of the Book

This book aims at defining and studying the banking-insurance conglomerates in the EU, determining their linkages with the new member states and their impact on new member states. The book provides a survey on banking and insurance undertakings both in the EU and the new member states in order to examine the degree of financial conglomeration across those institutions. The book also aims to analyse the strategies used by some important EU banking-insurance conglomerates in their activities in the new member states and define the reasons of related bank/insurance mergers.

In order to accomplish the objectives of the book, the following questions are evaluated:
- What are the major benefits, driving factors and risks of financial conglomeration?
- Which major EU banks and insurance undertakings form parts of banking-insurance groups and how significant are the largest EU banks and insurance undertakings?
- What are the major banking-insurance groups in the EU?
- What major developments of banking-insurance consolidation has the EU faced in recent years?
- What are the largest banks and insurance undertakings in the new member states?
- Which EU banking-insurance groups have established linkages with the new member states and of which nature are those linkages?
- How significant are the EU-linked banking-insurance groups in the new member states?
- What are the main developments and reasons of EU banking-insurance groups' M&A activities across the financial institutions of the new member states?

---

[2] The new member states are the 10 former accession countries which joined the European Union on 1 May 2004.

- What are the main opportunities and threats of banking-insurance conglomeration across borders?

Methodology

The book is mainly based on data of the year-end 2001. The data was obtained through 2003. The book focuses only on banking and insurance businesses which form parts of financial groups and does not look at other financial businesses (e.g. investment firms, securities houses, etc). I have chosen to separate the two types of institutions from the rest of financial services and examine only banking and insurance firms because the data suggest that financial conglomeration is largely based on the combination of these two activities. Thus, the examination of banking and insurance businesses provides comprehensive overview of the overall situation in financial conglomeration. In order to look at the linkages only, I do not intend to examine the regulatory thresholds for individual banking-insurance groups. In this book the term "bank(ing)-insurance group" is used for all financial groups, which comprise of both banks (banking activities) and insurance undertaking(s).

Different sources of data have been used in the completion of the book. The analytical information and discussion provided in the book are based on leading banking business editions, working papers, presentations and articles. I have also used central banks' publications and financial legislation.

Based on market, sector and company data, the book provides a survey on banking-insurance conglomeration. In the completion of the survey, I have used statistical information provided by local competent institutions (e.g., bankers' associations), central banks, supervisory authorities and international organisations (e.g., Comité Européen des Assurances). The data provided by banks and insurance companies have proven to be a useful source of information in the completion of analyses, tables and graphic explanations of the book. I have collected data from the Internet, annual reports, activity reports and publications of the institutions. I have also gained useful knowledge on financial conglomeration issues during my internship at the European Central Bank. The statements and arguments drawn in the survey are supported by a variety of tables and graphs.

Outline of the Book

The book consists of three chapters. The first chapter focuses on both the economic and legal aspects of financial conglomeration. The chapter explains the nature and characteristics of financial conglomeration, identifying different conglomerate structures and elements. The chapter argues why financial conglomeration is favoured, seeking to introduce trends and developments of financial conglomeration and rationale behind conglomeration (and related M&A activities). Additionally, the most important driving factors and economics of conglomeration are addressed. In this chapter, I also look at risk factors related to financial conglomeration.

The second chapter provides a survey on banking-insurance conglomeration in the EU. The chapter identifies the largest banks and insurance firms, seeking to define the linkages between them and whether they belong to a banking-insurance group. The chapter also seeks to determine the importance of the largest banks and insurance businesses correspondingly in European banking and insurance markets. Based on the survey, I finally identify major banking-insurance groups in the EU.

The last chapter provides a survey on banking-insurance conglomeration linkages between the EU and the new member states. The chapter determines the largest banks and insurance businesses within these new member states. In order to define financial conglomeration linkages between the EU and the new member states, the chapter identifies whether the largest banks and insurance undertakings in the new member states form parts of some EU-originated banking-insurance groups. In order to determine the significance of EU banking-insurance groups, the survey views some major financial characteristics of individual EU-linked banks and insurance firms in the new member states relative to the banking and insurance markets in these countries. I examine activity strategies of some selected EU banking-insurance groups in the new member states, defining the main forms of cross-border expansion and seeking to address some merger motives of the groups. Finally, the analysis of this chapter results in conclusions on potential opportunities and pitfalls of EU banking-insurance conglomeration across the borders of the new member states.

Acknowledgements

The book was initially prepared as my master's thesis at J. W. Goethe Frankfurt University, Institute for Law and Finance. The research provided in the second part of this book is based on my previous research work at the European Central Bank, Directorate Financial Stability and Supervision where I provided temporary research assistance to Mr. Frank Dierick in preparation of the occasional paper "The supervision of mixed financial services groups in Europe" (published in August 2004). My involvement in such an extensive and unique research project at the European Central Bank has been of great value for preparing this book. However, all the errors and omissions of the book are mine and my views expressed herein do not necessarily reflect those of the European Central Bank.

There are many who deserve my thanks for helping me write this book. My promoter, Prof. Paul Berndt Spahn for his advice and recommendations related to the development of my ideas and analysis provided in the book. I thank my former colleagues at the European Central Bank—Mr. Frank Dierick, Mr. Pedro Teixeira and Mrs. Ines Cabral—for their kind help and guidance. My knowledge and experience gained from many discussions on financial conglomeration issues, my colleagues' assistance and explanations in the field of data collection, handling and analysis have proven to be inevitably necessary for the completion of this book. And as with my many other papers and achievements, I owe the biggest thanks to my Mum, Urve, my family and friends for their ongoing support and encouragement to me.

Chapter 1

Financial Conglomeration: Economic and Legal Aspects

1.1. Nature and Features of Financial Conglomeration

Conglomeration can be defined as the combination of different activities, with more or less industrial synergies, under a common "financial umbrella." The keyword for conglomeration is diversification and usually the more diversified firms are considered to be conglomerates rather than the firms that are "focused."[1] Nevertheless, since the degree of diversification within a firm is a continuous variable, determining at what level a corporation has become a conglomerate is somewhat a matter of definition.[2]

Financial services integration involves the production or distribution of a financial service traditionally associated with one of the three major sectors by actors in another sector.[3] Conglomeration is a process leading to the creation of a group of financial companies operating in different sectors of the financial industry. There are three major areas of financial services: traditional banking, insurance and securities-related activities. Conglomeration is thus associated with the potential conduct of a range of financial services comprising of traditional banking (deposit-taking and lending), securities-related activities (such as trading of financial

---

[1] "Focused" firms are generally interpreted as firms that represent move-away from conglomeration, with less diversification of activities of different industrial segments in which the firms operate.

[2] National Bank of Belgium. *Financial Conglomerates.* Financial Stability Review, 2002, p. 61.

[3] H. D. Skipper Jr., *Financial Services Worldwide: Promises and Pitfalls.* Georgia State University, 2000, pp. 3–4. Available:
http://www.worldbank.org/wbi/banking/insurance/contractual/pdf/skipper.pdf

instruments and their derivatives, underwriting of new debt and equity issues, brokerage, investment management) and insurance.[4]

A financial conglomerate, as it is defined in the European Union, has four major characteristics:

a) a financial conglomerate is a *special group* of activities;
b) a financial conglomerate has at least *one regulated entity*[5] in the group (either at the head of the group or as a subsidiary);
c) the activities of a financial conglomerate are *mainly financial*, in those cases when the conglomerate is headed by a non-EU regulated entity or a non-regulated entity (e.g. mixed financial holding company);
d) a financial conglomerate has a *significant combined involvement* either in the banking *and insurance sector* or in the investment services *and insurance sector*.[6]

Thus, under the European framework, it is at least theoretically possible (although very unlikely in practice) that there is a group of activities that qualifies as a financial conglomerate without having a credit institution in a group.

Their structural forms describe financial conglomerates as special groups. A special group in the European Union has two structural options: it is formed either as a group of undertakings, which consists of a parent undertaking, its subsidiaries and includes participations,[7] or it represents a horizontal structure of undertakings linked to each other by a relationship within the meaning of the Directive 83/349/EEC.[8] A finan-

---

[4] R. Vander Vennet, "Cost and Profit Efficiency of Financial Conglomerates and Universal Banks in Europe." *Journal of Money*, Credit and Banking, vol. 34/1 February 2002, p. 260.

[5] According to the EU legislation, a regulated entity means a credit institution, an insurance undertaking or an investment firm, in all cases with their head office in the EU. In general, regulated entity consists of those undertakings of financial sector that are covered by specific sector rules and regulations.

[6] Directive 2002/87/EC, Art. 2 (14).

[7] According to the Directive 2002/87/EC of 16 December 2002 (Art. 2) the participation in entity means that the parent undertaking of the group or its subsidiaries hold ownership, directly or by way of control, of 20% or more of the voting rights or capital of an entity.

[8] Generally, in the horizontal group relationship there is no common parent company but the entities are managed on a unified basis as defined in Art. 12(1) of 7th Directive 83/349/EEC of 13 June 1983 based on Art. 54 (3) (g) of the Treaty on Consolidated Accounts, OJ L193, 18/07/1983, pp. 001–0017.

cial conglomerate may also be a sub-group of another financial conglomerate.[9]

There are different ways of identifying frequently used structural models for financial conglomerates. Financial conglomerates are generally organised according to one of the three distinct structural forms. One approach is the universal bank model, in which all financial operations are conducted within one single corporate entity. In this model, any separation of activities into separate entity reflects pure business considerations and not any regulatory limitations. The second model is a parent–subsidiary model or operating subsidiary model, in which operations are regulated as subsidiaries of another financial institution, usually but not necessarily a bank.[10] There are legal requirements for separate legal entities and the institutions may not capture the complete synergies available from diversification in a conglomerate structure. Thus, the assets of a regulated parent are generally protected from the problems of its subsidiary, except in the cases of corporate veil piercing, reputation damage or creditor–debtor relationship between a parent and its subsidiary.[11] The third model is a holding company model in which activities are conducted in legally distinct entities. All those entities, having separate capital and management, are owned by a single financial or non-financial unregulated entity, which is often seen as an "umbrella" organisation for financial activities.[12]

Another way to classify the structures of financial conglomerates is related to the difference between different countries. The most common structural forms of financial conglomerates are recognised accordingly: United States (hereinafter "U.S.") style financial holding company structure, United Kingdom (hereinafter "U.K.") style bank holding company structure and German (or French) style universal bank structure. U.S. style holding structure consists of a financial services holding company

---

[9] Directive 2002/87/EC, Art. 2 (13), (14).

[10] C. Half, "Evolving Trends in the Supervision of Financial Conglomerates: A Comparative Investigation of Responses to the Challenges of Cross-Sectoral Supervision in the United States, European Union, and United Kingdom." Harvard Law School: International Finance Seminar, April 30, 2002, p. 5.

[11] B. Shull, L. J. White, "The Right Corporate Structure for Expanded Bank Activities." *The Banking Law Journal*, 115 May 1998, No. 4, p. 474.

[12] C. Half, "Evolving Trends in the Supervision of Financial Conglomerates: A Comparative Investigation of Responses to the Challenges of Cross-Sectoral Supervision in the United States, European Union, and United Kingdom." Harvard Law School: International Finance Seminar, April 30, 2002, pp. 5–6.

that performs as a holding for separate financial activities. U.K. style bank holding company structure has the following arrangement: a commercial bank performs as a parent company for insurance, investment banking and other financial services. German or French universal banking conglomerate is usually formed by a universal bank as a parent company and insurance undertaking and other financial services firms as its subsidiaries.[13] There is no common understanding on the best structure. The choice among conglomerate structures is obviously driven both by regulatory and commercial reasons, but also depends much on such factors as system and practice in a particular country.

Financial conglomerates should be distinguished from industrial groups with relatively minor financial activities. Regarding groups headed by a non-regulated entity, a distinction between groups, which focus mainly on financial activities and those with wider ambit, can be made by identifying the groups' activities as "mainly financial."[14] For the purposes of determining the scope of activities (and providing criteria for identifying a group as a financial conglomerate), three important characteristics are set by the European Union legislation[15]:

a) *financial sector balance sheet threshold* –
   in order to determine whether the activities of a group are mainly financial, the ratio of balance sheet total of all financial sector[16] entities in the group should exceed 40 % of balance sheet total of the whole group;

b) *micro-economic parameter* –
   in order to determine whether the cross-sector financial activities of a group are significant, for each financial sector in the group:

---

[13] H. D. Skipper Jr., Financial Services Worldwide: Promises and Pitfalls. Georgia State University, 2000, pp. 5–7. Available: http://www.worldbank.org/wbi/banking/insurance/contractual/pdf/skipper.pdf

[14] European Commission, Internal Market Directorate General. *Towards an EU Directive on the Prudential Supervision of Financial Conglomerates: Consultation Document*, MARKT/3021/00-EN, 2000, p. 13.

[15] Directive 2002/87/EC, Art. 3.

[16] According to the Directive 2002/87/EC of 16 December 2002 (Art. 2) financial sector means a sector composed of one or more of the following entities: any banking industry undertaking covered by the scope of Directive 2000/12/EC (banking sector), any insurance undertaking covered by the scope of Directive 98/78/EC (insurance sector), any investment undertaking covered by the scope of Directive 93/6/EEC (investment services sector) and/or a mixed financial holding company within the meaning of Directive 2002/87/EC.

> the average ratio of the balance sheet total of that financial sector to the balance sheet total of all financial sector entities in the group
>
> AND
>
> the ratio of solvency requirements of the same financial sector to the total solvency requirements of all financial sector entities in the group

should exceed 10%

c) *macro-economic parameter* –
   - cross-sector activities are presumed to be significant if the balance sheet total of each financial sector in the group exceeds EUR 6 billion,
   - if micro-economic parameter equals to or is less than 10 %, and if inclusion of the group in the scope of the regulation of financial conglomerates is not necessary or would be inappropriate or misleading with respect to the objectives of supplementary supervision, a waiver may be granted by relevant competent authorities.

1.2. Why Financial Conglomeration?

1.2.1. Developments of Conglomeration

In the development of conglomeration as such, a rise in financial conglomerates versus vanishing general conglomerates can be noticed. Due to different factors—the deregulation of financial intermediation, the elimination of cross-border capital controls, better regulation on transparency and corporate governance—capital market efficiency has increased in recent years. These trends have reduced the need for general conglomerates as a way to get around capital market inefficiencies. Improved capital market efficiency can be assumed to lead some financial institutions to form financial conglomerates. While improvements in capital markets lower the diversification benefits for financial conglomerates just as for general conglomerates, these changes imply additional effects on banks (e.g. opportunities to offer more complex products, to exploit advanced technologies). These developments increase banks' incentives to form conglomerates.[17] Country specifics suggest a higher presence of general conglomerates in Continental Europe. Capital markets in Continental Europe are less efficient than in Anglo-Saxon countries and the presence of conglomerates in Anglo-Saxon countries is much lower. This trend can be explained by the more important role of "large block-holders" as the preferred corporate governance arrangement in Continental Europe, while dispersed stock ownership being more prevalent in Anglo-Saxon countries.[18]

Consolidation has been a global phenomenon in the financial services industry, leading to the conclusion that it is not only related to the effects of single market policy but rather to more intense global competition and the need to increase efficiency and reduce costs. The intensification of organisational links between banks and insurance companies has characterised the developments in the banking industry in many EU countries.[19] The combination of banking and insurance flies under various flags: "bancassurance", "allfinanz" and so on.[20]

The transformation process of banking sectors throughout the world is marked by the expansion of the banks' non-interest income, a rise in off-balance sheet relative to on-balance sheet activities, increased use of traded (and quite sophisticated) financial instruments and a broadening of activities to include securities and insurance.[21] With this shift in focus, the risks of traditional banks have changed. In addition to traditional credit risk, such financial conglomerates are now exposed to substantial market risk through their investment services arms. The trends also reflect asset management activities having become a major source of earnings throughout the financial sector.[22]

On one hand, consolidation across more distant and different types of financial institutions reflects the ongoing deregulation around the

[17] National Bank of Belgium. *Financial Conglomerates.* Financial Stability Review, 2002, p. 69.

[18] National Bank of Belgium. *Financial Conglomerates.* Financial Stability Review, 2002, p. 62.

[19] European Central Bank. *Banking in the Euro Area: Structural Features and Trends,* April 1999, pp. 46, 48.

[20] A. Leach, "European Bancassurance." *Financial Times,* London, 1993.

[21] National Bank of Belgium. *Financial Conglomerates.* Financial Stability Review, 2002, p. 64.

[22] S. R. Freedman, "Regulating the Modern Financial Firm: Implications of Disinter-mediation and Conglomeration." University of St. Gallen, Discussion Paper No. 2000–21, Sept. 2000, p. 15.

world. The idea of a single market within the European Union has supported deregulation, one of its main expressions—"single passport"[23]—having created more flexibility for cross-border financial operations.[24] Although "single passport" applies to the same financial sector, it has contributed to the growth of cross-border activities that allow institutions to become familiar with target countries and consider expansion into other financial sectors. On the other hand, the trends of technological and financial developments also seem to have created perfect conditions for ongoing consolidation. Improvements in information processing, telecommunications and financial technologies have facilitated greater geographic reach by allowing institutions to manage larger information flows and risks at lower cost without being geographically close to the customer. However, while there has been considerable consolidation within individual industrialised nations in recent years, cross-border mergers and acquisitions among these nations have generally been less frequent.[25]

Trends in cross-border provision of financial services also reflect reduction in trade barriers and declines in transportation costs that have led to the acceleration of international economic integration. The recent increase in international commerce facilitates a demand for international financial services which can be provided either directly by a financial institution from its home country, via syndicates originated by another financial institution in a foreign country or by a financial institution in the foreign country. Financial institutions can obtain physical presence abroad by acquiring foreign financial institutions (M&A) or by opening their own branches/subsidiaries there.[26] The evidence on EU institutions suggests that international expansion has mainly occurred by way of set-

---

[23] Single passport creates freedom for authorised financial service providers in one member state to go across borders of other member states with minimum hindrance. Authorisation is based on mutual recognition principle and authorisation in one member state creates the automatic passage to other member states.

[24] P. Molyneux, Y. Altunbas, E. Gardener, *Efficiency in European Banking*. John Wiley & Sons, 1996, pp. 32, 49.

[25] Federal Reserve System of the U.S. *To What Extent Will the Banking Industry Be Globalised? A Study of Bank Nationality and Reach in 20 European Nations*. International Finance Discussion Papers, May 2002, No. 725. Available:

http:// www.federalreserve.gov/pubs/ifdp

[26] A. N. Berger, R. De Young, H. Genay, G. F. Udell, "Globalisation of Financial Institutions: Evidence from Cross-Border Banking Performance." *Brookings-Wharton Papers on Financial Services*, 2000, Vol. 3, p. 6.

ting up new enterprises and through M&A activities in a rather balanced way.[27]

An important global trend in financial services industry has been increased substitutability between various types of financial instruments. This has implied that the demarcation lines between different financial services and intermediaries have become highly indistinct for both customers and producers.[28] It can be assumed that over time the fast-changing variety of financial services has altered the supply and demand for various financial services with providers seeking for more profitability and with customers becoming more sophisticated.

Banks are seen as major elements (and generally the centre) of financial conglomerates. Thus, the developments in banking play an important role in conglomerate formation. There have been several important and widely shared developments of the banking industry in the EU. First, banks tended to operate in accordance with the universal banking principle. This principle encompasses two elements: banks may engage in a full range of securities activities in a direct way rather than through separately incorporated subsidiaries and banks may closely link themselves to non-bank firms, by either equity holdings or board participation. Germany and Sweden are the best examples of such systems. The second feature of the EU banking industry is that there has been a fairly high level of government involvement. The relatively widespread public ownership of banks, especially in Germany, Italy, Spain and France, was reduced by important privatisation in the late 1980s. Restrictions on bank ownership of insurance companies were generally binding, especially in Belgium, France and the Netherlands. Regulations were even more constraining on insurance companies holding equity stakes in banks.[29]

The developments of banking and insurance connections in the EU differ among countries, reflecting country specifics and corresponding with overall global changes in financial services industry. In Belgium, for example, consolidation began influencing the banking industry around the middle of the 1990s. As a result of large mergers, the number of large banks declined and concentration increased towards the end of the dec-

---

[27] European Central Bank. *Mergers and Acquisitions Involving the EU Banking Industry – Facts and Implications*, December 2000, p. 15.

[28] S. Claessens, *Benefits and Costs of Integrated Financial Services Provision in Developing Countries.* University of Amsterdam and CEPR, 14 November 2002, p. 7.

[29] Group of Ten. *Report on Consolidation in the Financial Sector.* January 2001, pp. 47–54. Available: http://www.bis.org

ade. Consolidation has similarly influenced Belgian insurance industry. Quite differently, the developments in France reflect extensive privatisation (e.g., Société Générale and Banque Nationale de Paris in 1993, Crédit Lyonnais in 1999). State-owned mutual and co-operative banks were particularly prominent among the specialised banks. French banks could operate insurance companies, but faced very restrictive rules regarding starting up and acquiring equity stakes in such firms. After the liberalisation brought about by the single European market, evolution towards universal banking was further reinforced by a greater involvement of banks in life insurance activities (i.e. bancassurance). In the Netherlands, the process of liberalisation and deregulation resulted in allowing the mergers of universal banks that provided an array of services in commercial banking, investment banking and insurance. The insurance industry exhibited a historically close relationship to banking, with bancassurance taking off quite early in the Netherlands as compared to other countries.[30]

In Germany, banks have traditionally been free to operate as universal banks, but some restrictions required the separation of banking and insurance. Nonetheless, banks have collaborated with insurance companies primarily through strategic alliances and, to a lesser extent, cross-participation. Germany has had a tradition of cross-shareholdings between banks and insurance companies. As a result, banks chose to collaborate with insurance companies rather than develop in-house bancassurance. Similar to Germany, the Spanish financial sector is characterised by universal banking, whereby banking groups include firms that engage in insurance, asset management and securities activities. Banks can also hold equity stakes in non-financial companies. On the other hand, in Sweden, banking and insurance have, for a long time, traditionally remained separate. Only in the early 1990s were banks and insurance companies allowed to own shares in each other and become part of the same holding company.[31]

[30] Group of Ten. *Report on Consolidation in the Financial Sector.* January 2001, pp. 47–54. Available: http://www.bis.org

[31] Group of Ten. *Report on Consolidation in the Financial Sector.* January 2001, pp. 47–54. Available: http://www.bis.org

1.2.2. Reasons for Conglomeration

1.2.2.1. Motives of Financial Institutions

Traditionally, the decisions on going across borders and institutions are mainly affected by institution-specific factors and location-specific factors.[32] The main discussion of the benefits of financial conglomeration usually focuses on two aspects: whether combining banking with other financial services enables the potential creation of diversified businesses able to offer superior risk-return performance to that of more specialised firms; and the extent to which it is possible to segregate a financial conglomerate into legally distinct business units, thereby containing risk within individual operating units and preventing contagion between financially troubled and healthier units of a conglomerate. Now I will examine motives and external driving forces of conglomeration and related M&A activities, followed by the discussion of risks and safeguards of conglomeration in the last part of this chapter.

Conglomerates are most often formed in order to take advantage of revenue diversification. Both financial and general conglomerates may create value through diversification or through exploiting synergies. Similarly, they may destroy value through cross-subsidisation of unprofitable divisions.[33] Synergy literally means the process of working together. It is the 2-plus-2-equals-5 effect and is something that drives most M&A activities. Synergy most often indicates complement-driven mergers in which candidates give each other some previously "missing" element.[34] Generally financial services integration makes economic sense if it leads to the reduction in costs and increase in revenues. A reduction in costs is possible through economies of scale, economies of scope in production and operational efficiencies. All these factors suggest integration in production. On the other hand economies of scope in consumption and market power suggest integration in distribution and drive an increase in revenues.[35]

---

[32] C. M. Buch, "Why Do Banks Go Abroad?—Evidence from German Data." *Kiel Working Paper No. 948*, p. 8.

[33] National Bank of Belgium. *Financial Conglomerates.* Financial Stability Review, 2002, p. 61.

[34] S. Foster Reed, A. Reed Lajoux, *The Art of M&A: A Merger/Acquisition/Buyout Guide.* McGraw-Hill Companies, New York, 1998, p. 27.

[35] H. D. Skipper Jr., *Financial Services Worldwide: Promises and Pitfalls.* Georgia State University, 2000, pp. 8–11. Available:

   http://www.worldbank.org/wbi/banking/insurance/contractual/pdf/skipper.pdf

In principle, the decision to a merger or to acquire a firm should be motivated by the desire to increase the wealth of shareholders of the acquiring firm.[36] Individual transactions can be motivated by offensive (market penetration, diversification) and defensive (cost saving) objectives. Both types of motives can be socially beneficial. Offensive mergers may result in greater competition because of the firms striving to gain higher market shares. Defensive mergers may result in reduced excess capacity and lower prices.[37] Mergers are usually strategic (i.e. based on longer-term perspectives of enterprise development) or financial (i.e. based on fast-fulfilling financial expectations). Mergers that aim at conglomeration are usually of strategic kind.[38] The most common motives of institutions behind M&A activities and conglomeration are discussed as follows.

Cost efficiencies

Cost efficiencies generally appear in the form of cost-based economies of scale or cost-based economies of scope. In case of cost-based economies of scale, efficiency is achieved by lowering average cost per unit of output through expanding a single line of business. In case of cost-based economies of scope, efficiency is achieved by offering a broad range of products or services to a customer base.[39]

Conglomeration can lead to reductions in costs for a variety of reasons. Economies of scope in production exist if multiple products can be produced at less cost than the sum of the costs of producing each separately. Economies of scope could come about from (i) investment operations (having a single investment unit for all sectors), (ii) information technology (having customer information consolidated and available for multiple uses), (iii) distribution (using distribution channels established for one sector to sell other products), and (iv) reputation (having the good

---

[36] J. Dermin, "European Banking: Past, Present and Future." Conference Paper for the Second ECB Central Banking Conference, Frankfurt am Main, 24 and 25 October 2002, p. 27.

[37] I. Cabral, F. Dierick, J. Vesala, "Banking Integration in the Euro Area." European Central Bank, Occasional Paper No. 6. December 2002, p. 42.

[38] S. Foster Reed, A. Reed Lajoux, *The Art of M&A: A Merger/Acquisition/Buyout Guide.* McGraw-Hill Companies, New York, 1998, p. 15.

[39] J. Dermin, "European Banking: Past, Present and Future." Conference Paper for the Second ECB Central Banking Conference, Frankfurt am Main, 24 and 25 October 2002, pp. 27–28.

reputation of one firm, e.g., a commercial bank, enhance the sale of other conglomerate products).[40] On the consumption side, the potential for lower information, transaction and monitoring costs; better negotiation positions due to increased leverage; and lower price level in the situation of increased competition are the factors that lead to economies of scope.[41]

Cost synergies are revealed by economies of scope in the provision of multiple goods, but they may also include economies of scale (e.g. branch distribution networks, IT systems, risk management technology).[42] Cost economies from universal-type combinations[43] may be realised from (i) sharing physical inputs (e.g. offices, computer hardware); (ii) employing common information systems, investment departments, account service centres and other operations; (iii) obtaining capital by issuing public or private debt/equity in larger issue sizes that reduce the impact of fixed costs; and (iv) reusing managerial expertise and information.[44] The savings in case of achieving economies of scale would come from consolidating operations and eliminating redundant costs.[45] A larger scale production can lead to cost advantages through: (i) gains on concentration of risk management, administration functions, and integrated product development; (ii) marketing gains on common delivery of different services; (iii) better access and sharing of information; (iv) possibility to share reputation and pecuniary capital; and (v) enhanced potential for risk management through diversification gains.[46]

In terms of comparison of cost efficiencies among specialised institutions and financial conglomerates, it is interesting to note that there are

[40] H. D. Skipper Jr., *Financial Services Worldwide: Promises and Pitfalls.* Georgia State University, 2000, pp. 8–11. Available:

http://www.worldbank.org/wbi/banking/insurance/contractual/pdf/skipper.pdf

[41] S. Claessens, *Benefits and Costs of Integrated Financial Services Provision in Developing Countries.* University of Amsterdam and CEPR, 14 November 2002, pp. 13–14.

[42] National Bank of Belgium. *Financial Conglomerates.* Financial Stability Review, 2002, p. 68.

[43] Universal-type combinations reflect the effects of combinations among commercial banks, securities firms and insurance companies.

[44] A. N. Berger, R. De Young, H. Genay, G. F. Udell, "Globalisation of Financial Institutions: Evidence from Cross-Border Banking Performance." *Brookings-Wharton Papers on Financial Services,* 2000, Vol. 3, p. 12.

[45] R. A. Brealey, S. C. Myers, *Principles of Corporate Finance.* McGraw-Hill Companies, New York, 2003, p. 931.

[46] S. Claessens, *Benefits and Costs of Integrated Financial Services Provision in Developing Countries.* University of Amsterdam and CEPR, 14 November 2002, pp. 13–14.

relatively few empirical studies. The few existing mainly focus on universal banking efficiencies and provide different evidence in different aspects. The latest study of R. Vander Vennet suggests that the cost efficiency of financial conglomerates relative to the cost efficiency of specialised banks in traditional banking intermediation activities presents no advantage for financial conglomerates. However, conglomerates are found to be more cost efficient when non-traditional banking activities are taken into account.[47]

Revenue efficiencies
Revenue efficiencies are generally derived from revenue-based economies of scope and revenue-based economies of scale. The efficiency of revenue-based scope economies is expected from the cross-selling of new products to an already existing customer base. In the case of revenue-based economies of scale, size and large capital base will allow for generate efficiency.[48]

A financial conglomeration increases profits through economies of scope. Revenue synergies from cross-selling are supplemented by customer benefits from "one-stop shopping" and knowledge of individual customers that allows more accurate assessment of their product demand.[49] If each of the two firms has something the other needs, the two firms provide complementary resources through the merger.[50] Mergers which reduce the number of firms operating in one market (horizontal mergers) may lead to less competition and higher margins, while mergers across industries may generate higher profits by allowing the firms to package a bundle of goods.[51] Mergers may allow the dominant financial institution to enjoy the distribution of a range of products through a

---

[47] R. Vander Vennet, "Cost and Profit Efficiency of Financial Conglomerates and Universal Banks in Europe." *Journal of Money, Credit and Banking,* Vol. 34/1, Feb. 2002, p. 279.

[48] J. Dermin, "European Banking: Past, Present and Future." Conference Paper for the Second ECB Central Banking Conference, Frankfurt am Main, 24 and 25 October 2002, p. 28.

[49] National Bank of Belgium. *Financial Conglomerates.* Financial Stability Review, 2002, p. 68.

[50] R. A. Brealey, S. C. Myers, *Principles of Corporate Finance.* McGraw-Hill Companies, New York, 2003, p. 932.

[51] J. Dermin, "European Banking: Past, Present and Future." Conference Paper for the Second ECB Central Banking Conference, Frankfurt am Main, 24 and 25 October 2002, p. 29.

newly combined network system.[52] The broadening of a customer base through the merger is an important motivator as target firms could provide an outlet for the products of the new owner.[53] On the other hand, although mergers are mainly related to the expansion of services and certainly generate benefits for bidders, exploiting the benefits of market power may also create economic inefficiencies in general.

Cross-selling revenue scope economies may occur because of consumption complementarities arising from reductions in consumer search and transaction costs (e.g., one-stop shopping for commercial banking and insurance needs). Revenue economies may also occur due to sharing the reputation associated with recognised brand name.[54]

Cross-selling is related to the concept of one-stop shopping. One-stop shopping goes hand in hand with the deregulation and consolidation that have been sweeping the industry over the past few decades. One-stop shopping has several benefits in comparison to using multiple sources. The single source offers the advantage of convenience. The relational work in all the aspects is cut "in half" and so is the time. A single source can also offer a "holistic" perspective—if there has been a service provider–customer relationship for one service in the past, the service provider may have better ideas on how to deliver some other service to the customer and what the customer's needs are. Conversely, the customer may have a certain sense of loyalty to the service provider. The main drawback of one-stop shopping is a too extensive diversity. An institution might be doing a good job for a customer in one area, and a poor one in the other area. And even with relatively good service overall, no firm can possibly be the best in very different areas. A related concern is pricing: a customer that is "captive" for a number of services might not be as inclined to negotiate for lower prices. Finally, when institutions get involved in different fields, the possibilities for conflicts of interest grow proportionately.[55]

---

[52] P. Molyneux, Y. Altunbas, E. Gardener, *Efficiency in European Banking*. John Wiley & Sons, 1996, p. 223.

[53] D. Focarelli, F. Panetta, C. Salleo, "Why Do Banks Merge?" *Journal of Money, Credit and Banking*, October 2000, pp. 13–14.

[54] A. N. Berger, R. De Young, H. Genay, G. F. Udell, "Globalisation of Financial Institutions: Evidence from Cross-Border Banking Performance." *Brookings-Wharton Papers on Financial Services*, 2000, Vol. 3, p. 14.

[55] A. Reed Lajoux, J. F. Weston, *The Art of M&A Financing and Refinancing: A Guide to Sources and Instruments of External Growth*. McGraw-Hill Companies, New York, 1999, pp. 296–298.

Financial segments are melting into one another as financial institutions venture into diverse product markets (e.g., banks also sell insurance products and insurance firms sell unit-linked products) or offer innovative, mixed products (such as investment-based mortgages). New distribution channels, including the provision of financial services through the Internet, reinforce this effect. Hence, financial institutions' activities are becoming more varied but also generally more complex in nature.[56]

The combination of banking with insurance in particular (i.e. bancassurance) offers large economies of scope in terms of sales channels, product development, risk management and marketing.[57] The motives behind bancassurance vary. For banks, it is a means of product diversification and a source of additional fee income. Insurance companies see bancassurance as a tool for increasing their market penetration and premium turnover. Customers see bancassurance as a combination of reduced price, high quality products and doorstep delivery.[58]

When it comes to economies of scale, the increase in scale associated with consolidation may create revenue scale economies because some customers may need or prefer the services of larger institutions. A related revenue efficiency effect concerns the benefits from serving customers that operate in multiple nations, which often require or benefit from the services of financial institutions that operate in the same set of nations. Part of this revenue efficiency comes from financial institutions following their existing customers across international borders and maintaining the benefits of existing relationships.[59] Merging institutions could also achieve economies of scale in marketing activities, for example, product development and advertising.[60]

---

[56] I. van Lelyveld, A. Schilder, "Risk in Financial Conglomerates: Management and Supervision." Joint US–Netherlands Roundtable on Financial Services Conglomerates, Washington D.C., November 2002, Research Series Supervision, No. 49, pp. 5–6.

[57] S. Claessens, *Benefits and Costs of Integrated Financial Services Provision in Developing Countries.* University of Amsterdam and CEPR, 14 November 2002, p. 15.

[58] M. Kumar, "Bancassurance." *Financial Express,* 11 April 2000. Available: http://www.einsuranceprofessional.com/artbuzz.htm

[59] A. N. Berger, R. De Young, H. Genay, G. F. Udell, "Globalisation of Financial Institutions: Evidence from Cross-Border Banking Performance." *Brookings-Wharton Papers on Financial Services,* 2000, Vol. 3, p. 13.

[60] P. Molyneux, Y. Altunbas, E. Gardener, *Efficiency in European Banking.* John Wiley & Sons, 1996, p. 223.

Diversification and lower risk benefits
Financial conglomerates have diversification benefits, which arise from the following two sources. First, diversification makes the total profits of an integrated financial institution more stable than that of a financial institution specialised in a single product, given that the revenues of different business lines are not strongly correlated. Second, disintermediation has less influence on financial conglomerates. When companies bypass banks and use the forms of direct financing from public markets or when they obtain other types of financial products from non-bank service providers, the decline in lending (interest) business can be offset by an increase in other non-interest business (e.g., underwriting and placement).[61] In the EU, disintermediation has been favoured by the introduction of new technologies, financial liberalisation and Economic and Monetary Union. The disintermediation process has been more intense with regard to the diversification of savings, non-bank financial intermediaries having become relatively important in all EU countries.[62]

In terms of influence of disintermediation on financial conglomerates, the offsetting of activities may reduce incentives to engage in riskier business to maintain profits when faced with disintermediation. When it comes to risk diversification benefits, empirical studies suggest lower exposure to interest rate risk of a conglomerate that includes insurance activities.[63] Simulation studies[64] on risk diversification draw conclusions on different combinations of banking and non-bank financial services. The studies suggest that the banking-life insurance combination does not increase risk with respect to stand-alone banking and might actually lower risk. On the other hand, the results of studies on the combination of banking and securities or banking and property/casualty insurance unfortunately do not show any consistency.[65] Thus, it is important to interpret

---

[61] S. Claessens, *Benefits and Costs of Integrated Financial Services Provision in Developing Countries.* University of Amsterdam and CEPR, 14 November 2002, pp. 15–16.

[62] European Central Bank. *EU Bank's Income Structure.* Monthly Bulletin, April 2000, p. 7.

[63] S. Claessens, *Benefits and Costs of Integrated Financial Services Provision in Developing Countries.* University of Amsterdam and CEPR, 14 November 2002, pp. 15–16.

[64] In the U.S. different simulations (such as of Boyd and Graham (1998), Santomero and Chung (1992)) on financial mergers have been carried out in order to draw conclusions about possible effects on risk of mergers between banks and non-bank financial service providers. The simulations have used U.S. data.

[65] National Bank of Belgium. *Financial Conglomerates.* Financial Stability Review, 2002, p. 70.

the results of different studies with care and overall "binding" conclusions are difficult to be drawn from these studies.

Informational advantages

In order to make financing decisions of valuable investment projects, financial institutions need to gather firm-specific information. Gathering information and monitoring the project is costly. Financial conglomerates have the ability to provide a broader set of financial services than "focused" institutions and that allows them to use the information already gathered in providing one financial product in order to supply other financial services.[66] Thus, financial conglomerates clearly have the advantage of lower information and monitoring costs.

Because of the informational advantages, financial conglomerates are also able to design contracts that better suit the customer. Obviously informational advantages related to integrated financial services can be realised and passed on to the customers, but it depends in part on the level of informational asymmetries. In situations of low competition with weak information, banks are more likely to use their market power and retain the gains rather than pass them on.[67]

1.2.2.2. Driving Forces of Conglomeration

As previously discussed, the primary motives of institutions seem to be revenue enhancement and cost savings. Conglomeration and consolidation have also been encouraged by improvements in information technology, financial deregulation, globalisation of markets, and increased shareholder pressure for financial performance. A number of driving forces cause these motives to be effectual. First and foremost are the technological innovations in the field of information and communication technology, which paved the way for the development of many new products and drastically lowered the operational costs per unit. Large financial institutions are generally better able to fund the extensive investment in required information technology. Additionally, deregulation

---

[66] S. Claessens, *Benefits and Costs of Integrated Financial Services Provision in Developing Countries.* University of Amsterdam and CEPR, 14 November 2002, p. 18.

[67] S. Claessens, *Benefits and Costs of Integrated Financial Services Provision in Developing Countries.* University of Amsterdam and CEPR, 14 November 2002, pp. 18–19.

has opened plenty of new markets and allowed for new co-operative links (e.g. between banks and insurance companies). In practice, expansion and diversification are important tools in the strategic reorientation of financial institutions in response to mounting pressure, from both inside and outside the financial sector.[68]

When looking at exogenous factors and driving forces, it must be noted that macro-economic conditions and government policies in large measure shape the factors that affect M&A activity and conglomeration. Thus, the factors have cycles that may change significantly together with shifts in the world and domestic economies and changes in governmental policies.[69] Among the major forces creating pressure for change are technological advances, deregulation and globalisation of the marketplace.[70] These trends affect all financial sectors. For example, the European banking industry is increasingly exposed to the trends that are continuously opening doors for non-bank players in banking business.[71]

Improvements in information technology
Competitive intelligence—especially technology tracking—has become a major driving force behind M&A activity and conglomeration.[72] New technological developments have been very important to encourage consolidation because of their high fixed costs and the need to spread these costs across a large customer base. At the same time, dramatic improvements in the speed and quality of communications and information processing have made it possible for financial service providers to offer a broader array of products and services to larger numbers of clients over wider geographic areas than had been feasible in the past.[73]

---

[68] I. van Lelyveld, A. Schilder, "Risk in Financial Conglomerates: Management and Supervision." Joint US–Netherlands Roundtable on Financial Services Conglomerates, Washington D.C., November 2002, Research Series Supervision, No. 49, pp. 5–6.

[69] M. Lipton, *Mergers: Past, Present and Future*. Wachtell, Lipton, Rosen & Katz, 10 January 2001.

[70] Group of Ten. *Report on Consolidation in the Financial Sector,* January 2001, pp. 70–73. Available: http://www.bis.org

[71] J. de Larosière, E. Barthalon, *Banking Consolidation in Europe: Adapting to Financial Consolidation*. Routledge International Studies in Money and Banking, 2001, pp. 15–16.

[72] S. Foster Reed, A. Reed Lajoux, *The Art of M&A: A Merger/Acquisition/Buyout Guide*. McGraw-Hill Companies, New York, 1998, p. 921.

[73] Group of Ten. *Report on Consolidation in the Financial Sector*. January 2001, p. 65–69. Available: http://www.bis.org

However, technological advances as a driving factor for conglomeration and mergers should be seen in a long-term perspective. In the short run, technological development may sometimes even obstruct a merger, as merging incompatible systems can be very costly in the short-term. In the medium to long term, however, cost savings are achievable by the use of more efficient technologies and increasing cost of information technology might itself be a reason for conglomeration.[74]

Technology has both direct and indirect effects on the restructuring of financial services. Direct effects of technology may include (i) increases in the feasible scale of production of certain products and services (e.g. credit cards and asset management); (ii) scale advantages in the production of risk management instruments such as derivative contracts and other off-balance sheet guarantees; (iii) economies of scale in the provision of services such as custody, cash management, research, etc. M&A activity is often pursued as a means of spreading the high set-up costs of new technological infrastructure over a larger customer base. A large sized firm helps to counterbalance competitive pressures and provides for the continuous technology upgrades necessary to achieve any unit-cost advantage in pricing services that are basically commodity products.[75]

Improvements in the speed and quality of telecommunications, computers and information services have helped to lower information and other costs of transacting. This development has had an impact on the financial services industry by:

a)   changes in distribution capacity in terms of a broader array of products, a larger number of clients and wider geographic areas;

b)   creation of new financial services and products in terms of better ability to unbundle and repackage the risks embedded in existing financial products to tailor to new products which meet the risk management and investment needs of specific customers;

c)   blurring of distinctions in terms of both intra-sector and inter-sector competition (e.g., banks increasingly engage in non-traditional activities);

d)   data mining which means that differentiated or specially tailored products can be created and channelled to targeted customers; and

---

[74] European Central Bank. *The Effects of Technology on the EU Banking System.* July 1999, p. 31.

[75] Group of Ten. *Report on Consolidation in the Financial Sector.* January 2001, pp. 70–73. Available: http://www.bis.org

e)   new entrants without the need for a pre-existing physical presence.[76]

Government policy and deregulation

Government policy can play an important role in both facilitating or hindering conglomeration and consolidation. Governments sometimes facilitate consolidation in an effort to minimise the social costs associated with firm failures, they may also promote consolidation in an effort to create a national company that can compete in the global arena. Government policy is mainly related to the establishment and developments of favourable or less favourable regulation and policy decisions that have influence on cross-border mergers and financial consolidation. The most important fields of regulation are those related to accounting, competition issues, taxation and labour law.

Accounting rules may create good pre-conditions and set a favourable regime for certain aspects of M&A activities (e.g. amortisation of goodwill by pooling accounting for merger). The scope of the protection of fair competition determines whether antitrust regulators promote, retard or prohibit mergers. Promoting mergers is a factor that allows mergers and thereby treats merger as a positive action. Thus, positive merger-regulation is a strong driving factor.[77] At the same time, laws requiring regulatory approval of mergers and acquisitions or prohibiting certain types of mergers and acquisitions (because of their implications for competition, financial stability, potential conflicts of interest between commercial and investment banking, or other reasons) have the potential to hinder consolidation.[78]

When taxation law has a driving effect on mergers, I believe it is mainly an indirect effect. It is evidently not about tax-beneficial treatment for certain transactions, but about the fact that certain tax provisions have certain economic effect and that effect triggers mergers (e.g., when the tax law facilitates banks selling their significant stakes in companies, the tax law is a potential stimulant to new mergers). Labour laws aim at employee protection, employee resistance to mergers depends on the general prosperity and employment rate.[79]

---

[76] Group of Ten. *Report on Consolidation in the Financial Sector.* January 2001, pp. 70–73. Available: http://www.bis.org

[77] M. Lipton, *Mergers: Past, Present and Future.* Wachtell, Lipton, Rosen & Katz, 10 January 2001.

[78] Group of Ten. *Report on Consolidation in the Financial Sector.* January 2001, pp. 65–69. Available: http://www.bis.org

[79] M. Lipton, *Mergers: Past, Present and Future.* Wachtell, Lipton, Rosen & Katz, 10 January 2001.

Government and public policy determine the macro-economic conditions under which a state functions and those conditions might have an effect on mergers and conglomeration. An important issue is monetary decisions. For example, fluctuations in currencies have impact on cross-border M&A, e.g. appreciation of one currency against the other leads to the increase of acquisitions by companies of the country with a strong currency in the country with a weak currency.[80]

Additionally, going abroad is strongly correlated with the degree of economic integration between the home country of an institution and the country where the investment is made.[81] Other location-specific factors such as the size of the foreign markets, trade relations and the presence of non-financial firms on the market influence the institutions' foreign direct investment decisions.[82] Population density may also be important to an acquirer seeking economies of scale, because in the countries with a less spread population it is easier to build up a branch network.[83]

World-wide deregulation is an important driving force of consolidation and conglomeration. Governments influence the process through effects on market competition and entry conditions (e.g., placing limits on or prohibiting cross-border mergers or mergers between banks and other types of service providers). They also have influence through approval/disapproval decisions for individual merger transactions, through limits on the range of permissible activities for service providers, through public ownership of institutions and efforts to minimise the social costs of failures. Financial regulatory frameworks in major countries have shifted from systems based on strict regulatory control to systems based more on enhancing efficiency through competition, with an emphasis on market discipline, supervision and risk-based capital guidelines. In the new operating environment, public policy is less protective of financial service providers (banks), exposing them to the same sorts of market pressures that have long confronted non-financial businesses. The main influence

[80] M. Lipton, *Mergers: Past, Present and Future.* Wachtell, Lipton, Rosen & Katz, 10 January 2001.

[81] D. Focarelli, A. F. Pozzolo, "The Determinants of Cross-Border Bank Shareholdings: an Analysis with Bank-Level Data from OECD Countries." Banca d'Italia, Temi di discussione del Servizio Studi, No. 381, October 2000, pp. 13–14.

[82] C. M. Buch, "Why Do Banks Go Abroad?—Evidence from German Data." The Kiel Institute of World Economics, Kiel Working Paper, No. 948, p. 8.

[83] C. M. Buch, G. L. DeLong, "Cross-Border Bank Mergers: What Lures the Rare Animal?" Kiel Working Paper No. 1070, August 2001, p. 9.

of deregulation appears to be that it enlarges the set of legal tactical manoeuvres, including the types of agreements that can be arranged across sectors and across borders, and thereby gives institutions increased flexibility to respond to competitive impulses.[84] Within the EU, the creation of the euro area is seen to have played a role in intra-EU mergers.[85]

Globalisation of the marketplace
Globalisation is, in many respects, a by-product of technological change and deregulation. Technological advances have lowered computing costs and telecommunications, while at the same time greatly expanding capacity and making a global reach economically more feasible. Deregulation, meanwhile, has opened up many new markets both in developed and in transition economies. Globalisation largely affects institutions providing wholesale services. As non-financial corporations have increased the geographical scope of their operations, they have created a demand for intermediaries to provide products and services attuned to the international nature of their operations. Maintaining presence in multiple financial markets and offering a breadth of products and services can entail relatively high fixed costs, thus creating a need for large size to achieve scale economies. Additionally, M&A activities have been a frequent option for banks seeking to build a global retail system. Globalisation has also helped change the competitive dynamics of other market segments, as national and regional players are forced to respond to the threat posed by new entrants either by offering better pricing or offering better services (e.g., personal service).[86]

1.2.2.3. Economics of Conglomeration

Having addressed the motives and driving factors of conglomeration, I have recognised that financial conglomeration from an institutions' perspective is highly efficiency-driven. Financial integration is economically logical if it results in the reduction of operating costs, an increase in revenues, or both. Stressing the difference in perspective between the previ-

---

[84] Group of Ten. *Report on Consolidation in the Financial Sector.* January 2001, pp. 70–73. Available: http://www.bis.org
[85] European Central Bank. *Mergers and Acquisitions Involving the EU Banking Industry—Facts and Implications.* December 2000, p. 19.
[86] Group of Ten. *Report on Consolidation in the Financial Sector.* January 2001, pp. 65–73. Available: http://www.bis.org

ous and following discussions on economies of scale and scope, I will now explore how the economics of conglomeration is generally understood and discuss whether conglomeration really is to bring efficiencies. I will address both cost effects and revenue effects.

Cost Effects
As previously explained, financial services conglomerates could enjoy cost advantages through realising economies of scale, economies of scope in production, or operational efficiencies. Economies of scale exist if the average cost of production falls with increased output, holding the product mix stable. Economies of scale in themselves would not seem to justify the formation of multi-sector financial firms, although they may justify existing conglomerates growing larger through organic growth or mergers or acquisitions. Skipper[87] has examined the results of several studies, which aim at defining the effects on cost efficiencies of economies of scale. The studies have found some evidence of scale economies for financial conglomerates, but not for very large institutions. The results of the studies indicate that the consensus seems to be that scale economies and diseconomies do not result in more than about 5 per cent difference in unit costs.

Economies of scope are likely to be important in the provision of financial services because of the ability to share overhead, technology, and other fixed costs across a range of products. Thus, the fixed costs of managing a client relationship would seem to lend themselves to sharing across a broad range of financial services. As with studies on economies of scale, most scope studies find that, where they exist, they are exhausted at fairly low levels of output. Diseconomies of scope are not unlikely. Financial conglomerates are large firms with substantial bureaucracies. They may suffer from inertia and an inability to respond quickly to changing markets and customer demand. They may lack creativity, realise internal compensation conflicts that erode synergy, and suffer from serious internal cultural differences across sectors that inhibit co-operation and co-ordination necessary for synergy. If integration yields positive cost effects through economies of scale or scope, one would expect to find conglomerates moving toward production and op-

[87] H. D. Skipper Jr., *Financial Services Worldwide: Promises and Pitfalls.* Georgia State University, 2000, pp. 8–11. Available:
http://www.worldbank.org/wbi/banking/insurance/contractual/pdf/skipper.pdf

erational integration. Back-office operations such as investment, accounting, information technology, risk management, and so on would more likely be the basis for realising economic gains. Synergies would likely relate to both the corporate and retail markets.[88]

Revenue Effects

Two aspects of financial integration can really rise to important revenue effects: market power and economies of scope in consumption. Large size can convey market power; i.e. the ability to affect price.[89] Thus, one of the rationales of M&A activities is that institutions might search for monopoly power.[90] This is particularly true when the merging firms are direct competitors and their combination results in a substantial increase in market concentration.[91] In exercising their market power, conglomerates would enhance their revenue (or at least profit) stream. As is already known, until the mid-1990s many countries strictly limited access to their financial services markets. With fewer barriers to entry, more competitive markets with fewer opportunities to gain market power evolve.

As we have seen, integration may enhance the earnings potential of a financial conglomerate through distribution of a greater product range. These economies of scope in consumption, i.e. the demand-side economies of scope could follow from the cross-marketing of products. Many financial products are complements (e.g., mortgage loans and mortgage protection life insurance policies). Customers could realise lower search, information, monitoring and transactions costs by purchasing products from a conglomerate than from specialised firms. If such consumption economies exist, customers presumably would be willing to pay more for products offered in this convenient way. If integration yields positive revenue effects through economies of scope in consumption, one would expect to find financial integration leaning more toward distribution but less is gained by production and operational integration. In such instances, bancassurance arrangements with or without affiliation, would be

---

[88] H. D. Skipper Jr., Financial Services Worldwide: Promises and Pitfalls. Georgia State University, 2000, pp. 8–11. Available:
http://www.worldbank.org/wbi/banking/insurance/contractual/pdf/skipper.pdf

[89] N. G. Mankiw, *Principles of Economics.* Harcourt College Publishers, 2001, p. 813.

[90] G. De Nicolo, *Consolidation, Conglomeration and Financial Risk: A Progress Report.* International Monetary Fund Mae Department, Presentation, July 2002.

[91] Group of Ten. *Report on Consolidation in the Financial Sector.* January 2001, pp. 65–69. Available: http://www.bis.org

sufficient. Synergies would likely relate more to the retail than to the corporate market.[92]

1.3. Risks and Safeguards of Financial Conglomeration

In previous parts of this chapter I have discussed why financial conglomeration might be favoured and what triggers mergers and conglomeration. From a supervisors' perspective, however, financial conglomeration entails several risks and the natural worry for supervisors is the extent to which conglomeration could weaken the safeguards put in place through regulatory requirements. Trends in financial conglomeration have resulted in financial authorities facing broadly similar policy issues:

a) the appropriate corporate structure of financial conglomerates in order to determine to what extent risks in the components of the conglomerate should be segregated by separate legal structures, separate capitalisation and "firewalls";

b) the scope on which the supervisory regime should be institutionally or functionally based and how to ensure competitive neutrality between financial conglomerates and specialised firms; and

c) the institutional structure of financial regulators and the degree to which the supervision of the various businesses in a conglomerate should be consolidated.

The general principle of group supervision is that authorities should monitor institutions' world-wide operations based on verifiable consolidated data, and the creation of corporate structures that impede consolidated supervision should be forbidden.[93] It must be emphasised that supplementary supervision of financial conglomerates does not mean supervision on a consolidated basis like the supervision provided by sectoral rules. For financial conglomerates a so-called solo-plus approach to supervision is followed. The basis of supervision is the supervision of individual group entities on a solo-basis by their respective regulators. The solo supervision of individual entities is complemented by a general

---

[92] H. D. Skipper Jr., *Financial Services Worldwide: Promises and Pitfalls.* Georgia State University, 2000, pp. 8–11. Available:
http://www.worldbank.org/wbi/banking/insurance/contractual/pdf/skipper.pdf

[93] J. Eatwell, L. Taylor, *Global Finance at Risk: The Case for International Regulation.* Polity Press, 2000, p. 199.

quantitative assessment of the group as a whole and, usually, by a quantitative group-wide assessment of capital adequacy.[94]

The supervision of financial conglomerates presents a challenge for supervisors on two distinct axes. The first of these is that of supervising activities in varying business lines, and accounting not only for the risks within each business but the potential impact of particular activities in the group as a whole, its soundness and its stability. The second major challenge facing supervisors is that of multinational co-ordination, as international financial conglomerates may be subject to potentially conflicting capital and other supervisory requirements across jurisdictions.[95]

In the following I will examine the major risks of financial conglomeration and discuss the safeguards against the problems of conglomeration. The set of potential problems of conglomeration can be divided into (i) regulatory arbitrage, (ii) internal contagion effects, (iii) complexity and lack of transparency effects, (iv) conflicts of interest, (v) market concentration and reduction of competition and (vi) unregulated entities.

Regulatory arbitrage

The two important forms of regulatory arbitrage are multiple gearing and excessive leveraging.[96] In the situation of multiple gearing the same own funds are used simultaneously as a buffer more than once, i.e. to cover the capital requirements of the parent company as well as those of a subsidiary.[97] As a result, the "net" solvency of the group is in fact less than the sum of the capital of the individual group components.[98] Excessive leveraging occurs when the conglomerate issues debt and gives the pro-

[94] M. Gruson, "Supervision of Financial Holding Companies in Europe: The Proposed EU Directive on Supplementary Supervision of Financial Conglomerates." J. W. Goethe University, Institut für Bankrecht, Working Paper No. 94, 2001, p. 16.

[95] H. E. Jackson, C. Half, "Background Paper on Evolving Trends in the Supervision of Financial Conglomerates." Conference Paper, 26 June 2002, pp. 8–9.

[96] National Bank of Belgium. *Financial Conglomerates.* Financial Stability Review, 2002, p. 74.

[97] M. Gruson, "Supervision of Financial Holding Companies in Europe: The Proposed EU Directive on Supplementary Supervision of Financial Conglomerates." J. W. Goethe University, Institut für Bankrecht, Working Paper No. 94, 2001, p. 16.

[98] C. Half, "Evolving Trends in the Supervision of Financial Conglomerates: A Comparative Investigation of Responses to the Challenges of Cross-Sectoral Supervision in the United States, European Union, and United Kingdom." Harvard Law School: International Finance Seminar, 30 April 2002, p. 15.

ceeds as equity to its regulated subsidiary.[99] Such arbitrage is particularly likely where the regulatory frameworks for banks and insurance firms differ in measuring risk and determining capital requirements.[100]

Apart from banks distributing insurance (insurance broking), the insurance activities of a bank are located in different members of a corporate group. This is because each activity must be separately capitalised. The regulatory regimes also differ. For example, the calculation of solvency varies fundamentally: with banks it is a function of the assets i.e. loans, etc. whereas with insurers it is a function of the risk that they may be called on to meet the liabilities of policyholders.[101] One significant difficulty in supervising financial conglomerates is that of calculating capital adequacy related to the potential problem within a conglomerate structure—multiple/(double)-gearing.[102] Safeguards against multiple gearing and excessive leverage function through the partial deduction from capital of the participation in subsidiaries.[103] The major goal of supplementary supervision on the capital adequacy of the regulated entities in a financial conglomerate is to eliminate any inappropriate intra-group creation of own funds. The solvency requirements of each separate financial sector in a financial conglomerate are to be covered by own fund elements in accordance with corresponding sectoral rules. Only own funds elements that are eligible as cross-sector capital qualify for the verification of the compliance with additional solvency requirements at the financial conglomerate level.[104]

The development of an effective supervisory regime for financial conglomerates may be particularly difficult for supervisors. Even where formal legal boundaries exist, management may be best able to capture the

[99] National Bank of Belgium. *Financial Conglomerates.* Financial Stability Review, 2002, p. 74.

[100] I. van Lelyveld, A. Schilder, "Risk in Financial Conglomerates: Management and Supervision." Joint US–Netherlands Roundtable on Financial Services Conglomerates, Washington D.C., November 2002, Research Series Supervision No. 49, pp. 9–10.

[101] R. Cranston, *Principles of Banking Law.* Oxford University Press, 1997, pp. 38–39.

[102] H. E. Jackson, C. Half, "Background Paper on Evolving Trends in the Supervision of Financial Conglomerates." Conference Paper, 26 June 2002, pp. 15–16.

[103] National Bank of Belgium. *Financial Conglomerates.* Financial Stability Review, 2002, p. 75.

[104] M. Gruson, "Supervision of Financial Holding Companies in Europe: The Proposed EU Directive on Supplementary Supervision of Financial Conglomerates." J. W. Goethe University, Institut für Bankrecht, Working Paper No. 94, 2001, pp. 16–17.

benefits of the conglomerate structure by operating the organisation as an integrated whole and adopting a co-ordinated perspective on risk management and resource allocation. Supervisors may justifiably be concerned with risk transfer within the conglomerate in order to ensure that the risks are transferred in a manner consistent with underlying regulatory concerns and motivations, and not as a means of evading or minimising supervisory requirements without any real change in economic risk.[105] A welfare-maximising regulator should attempt to discourage "gambling" in order to avoid risk-shifting as a form of moral hazard.[106]

Another core regulation is the requirement of supplementary supervision of intra-group transactions and risk-concentration of regulated entities. The presence of intra-group transactions and risk exposures within a financial group in not a matter of supervisory concern *per se*.[107] Intra-group transactions may cause supervisory concerns when they (i) result in capital or income being inappropriately transferred from the regulated entity, (ii) are on terms or under circumstances which parties operating at arm's length would not allow and may be disadvantageous to a regulated entity, (iii) can adversely affect the solvency, liquidity and profitability of individual entities within a group, or (iv) are used as a means of supervisory arbitrage, thereby evading capital or other regulatory requirements.[108]

Internal contagion effects
The risk of internal contagion is of the same type as the cross-subsidisation of bad divisions by good ones in general industrial conglomerates. An internal contagion risk could arise in a conglomerate in the form of transformation of negative effect from one business to another. For example, problems at the insurance end of the business drag down the capital resources of the sister bank. The higher the earnings

[105] H. E. Jackson, C. Half, "Background Paper on Evolving Trends in the Supervision of Financial Conglomerates." Conference Paper, 26 June 2002, pp. 15–16.
[106] A. D. Morrison, *The Economics of Capital Regulation in Financial Conglomerates.* Merton College and Said Business School, University of Oxford, August 2002, p. 4.
[107] European Commission, *Internal Market Directorate General. Towards an EU Directive on the Prudential Supervision of Financial Conglomerates: Consultation Document,* MARKT/3021/00-EN, 2000, p. 5. Available: http//europa.eu.int/comm/internal_market/finances/ cross-sector issues
[108] M. Gruson, "Supervision of Financial Holding Companies in Europe: The Proposed EU Directive on Supplementary Supervision of Financial Conglomerates." J. W. Goethe University, Institut für Bankrecht, Working Paper No. 94, 2001, pp. 21–22.

volatility of the business that is merged into a financial institution, the higher the risk of internal contagion. In case of bancassurance the effect is worsened, when the problems in the insurance arm translate into incentives to "gamble" with insured banking deposits.[109]

In previous parts of this chapter I have discussed that conglomeration may reduce risk through diversification benefits. However, this might not be the whole story. From risk management perspective, a conglomerate poses special challenges for both institutions and regulators. On the one hand, the challenge is to determine the standalone risk of an activity within a business line (e.g. credit risk in a commercial loan portfolio). On the other hand, the challenge is to combine the different risk factors within a business line (e.g. banks and insurance undertakings are subject to specific requirements).[110] While running several business lines might bring diversification advantages, there is a distinct possibility that the underlying correlations might increase significantly during crisis. Conglomerates that face distress in one of its components could easily be subject to intra-group contagion, as customers and investors involved with separate parts of the group lose confidence in the brand as a whole and difficulties are transferred to other parts of the conglomerate.[111] The problem is that as the integration of businesses of a financial conglomerate derives from the search for synergies, the group's situation reflects all its' businesses. Thus, localised problems could spread and affect the conglomerate as a whole on a wider scale.

As a safeguard, monitoring intra-group transactions is also an important factor in the case of dealing with the risk contagion within a financial conglomerate. The element of interdependence between the entities within the same financial conglomerate is crucial from a supervisory perspective.[112] Contagion entails the risk that, if certain parts of a conglom-

---

[109] National Bank of Belgium. *Financial Conglomerates.* Financial Stability Review, 2002, p. 74.

[110] A. Kuritzkes, T. Schuermann, S. M. Weiner, *Risk Measurement, Risk Management and Capital Adequacy in Financial Conglomerates.* The Wharton Financial Institutions Center, 2002, pp. 13–14.

[111] S. R. Freedman, "Regulating the Modern Financial Firm: Implications of Disintermediation and Conglomeration." University of St. Gallen, Discussion Paper No. 2000–21. September 2000, p. 20.

[112] European Commission, *Internal Market Directorate General. Towards an EU Directive on the Prudential Supervision of Financial Conglomerates: Consultation Document,* MARKT/3021/00-EN, 2000, p. 24. Available: http//europa.eu.int/comm/internal_market/finances/Cross-sector Issues

erate are experiencing financial difficulties, they may infect other healthy parts of the conglomerate. In identifying risk due to risk concentration, the different ways in which large losses can develop in a conglomerate as a result of risk concentration, have to be taken into account.[113] These possible contagion and cross-sector moral hazard risks form an argument for supervisory intervention at a financial conglomerate that would be stricter than the rules applying to its composing firms and that would also include supervisory requirements for non-regulated entities.[114]

Typical intra-group transactions (i.e. direct or indirect claims of units within a conglomerate that are held by other conglomerate units) include (i) credit extensions or lines of credit between affiliates, (ii) cross-shareholdings, (iii) intra-group trading in securities, (iv) insurance or other risk management services provided by one unit for another and (v) intra-group guarantees and commitments. Regulators must ensure that capital is increased or activities are limited if the risks that other company pose to the regulated entity appear to be unacceptable.[115]

Complexity and transparency

Financial conglomerates are complex in nature and very large. The structures of financial groups vary greatly because of tax, legal, cultural, regulatory and historical considerations. Complexity is multiplied within such groups. Complexity limits the ability of supervisors to comprehend and detect intra-group, related-party or other complex transactions, while difficulties in one part of a conglomerate usually have a knock-on effect on other components as well.[116] Associated with complexity, an important issue is the potential lack of transparency of accounts. Transparency concerns the extent to which accurate, complete, timely, and relevant information about the financial group is readily available to regulators, and sometimes also to other interested parties, such as customers, rating

---

[113] M. Gruson, "Supervision of Financial Holding Companies in Europe: The Proposed EU Directive on Supplementary Supervision of Financial Conglomerates." J. W. Goethe University, Institut für Bankrecht, Working Paper No. 94, 2001, pp. 21–22.

[114] I. van Lelyveld, A. Schilder, "Risk in Financial Conglomerates: Management and Supervision." Joint US–Netherlands Roundtable on Financial Services Conglomerates, Washington D.C., November 2002, Research Series Supervision No. 49, pp. 9–10.

[115] H. D. Skipper Jr., *Financial Services Worldwide: Promises and Pitfalls.* Georgia State University, 2000, pp. 44–46. Available:

http://www.worldbank.org/wbi/banking/insurance/contractual/pdf/skipper.pdf

[116] National Bank of Belgium. *Financial Conglomerates.* Financial Stability Review, 2002, p. 75.

agencies, etc. This form of transparency is often classified as disclosure.[117]

Regulators are concerned about the possibility of opaque management, ownership and legal structures. If supervisors do not fully understand these structures, they may be unable to properly assess either the totality of the risks faced by the group or the risk that unregulated members of the group may pose to the regulated members. Regulators are concerned that they might not be able to fully understand the lines of accountability relevant to their tasks. There is a concern that some groups may choose complex structures to make their operations opaque in order to avoid or impede effective regulation. To avoid these problems, regulators must have the power to secure needed information from the group itself or from other regulators.[118]

Regulation as a safeguard aims at limiting the problems linked to complexity and lack of transparency by insisting on proper risk management procedures and on tight co-operation between different supervisors.[119] Despite acceptable transparency, the size of financial conglomerates always generates additional systemic risks.[120] Ever larger conglomerates may become politically and economically very powerful.[121] Thus, conglomerates may easily become "too big to fail."

There is a moral hazard problem associated with the "too big to fail" position. It is assumed that institutions have more incentives to "gamble" when they know that due to their size and influence on systemic stability, authorities will help them in case of financial difficulties. In addition, it becomes more difficult to manage and understand the operation of a firm as the organisation grows.[122]

---

[117] H. D. Skipper Jr., *Financial Services Worldwide: Promises and Pitfalls.* Georgia State University, 2000, pp. 43–45. Available:

http://www.worldbank.org/wbi/banking/insurance/contractual/pdf/skipper.pdf

[118] H. D. Skipper Jr., *Financial Services Worldwide: Promises and Pitfalls.* Georgia State University, 2000, pp. 43–45. Available:

http://www.worldbank.org/wbi/banking/insurance/contractual/pdf/skipper.pdf

[119] National Bank of Belgium. *Financial Conglomerates.* Financial Stability Review, 2002, p. 75.

[120] H. E. Jackson, C. Half, "Background Paper on Evolving Trends in the Supervision of Financial Conglomerates." Conference Paper, 26 June 2002, pp. 17–18.

[121] S. Claessens, *Benefits and Costs of Integrated Financial Services Provision in Developing Countries.* University of Amsterdam and CEPR, 14 November 2002, p. 27.

[122] I. van Lelyveld, A. Schilder, "Risk in Financial Conglomerates: Management and Supervision." Joint US–Netherlands Roundtable on Financial Services Conglomerates, Washington D.C., November 2002, Research Series Supervision, No. 49, pp. 10–11.

Conflicts of interest

Financial conglomerates are found to come with potential conflicts of interest. In principle, the possibilities for conflicts of interest increase when financial institutions offer a wider array of products and have a broad set of customers. However, in the case of potential conflicts of interest, the critical issue is not whether they exist but rather whether the incentives and opportunities to exploit them exist. Market forces in general, such as competition from other financial institutions, reduce the incentives to exploit conflicts of interest, as do potential damage to reputation and the monitoring by creditors and non-market monitors, such as rating agencies. When these conditions prevail, conflicts of interest might be misused. In general, conflicts of interest tend to be more important in countries where disclosure rules are weak, information on financial institutions' activities is limited, and where competition is limited and supervision is weak.[123]

Market concentration and reduction of competition

Conglomeration may lead to greater market concentration by raising optimal scale of institutions and allowing greater linkages between different institutions. Thus, financial conglomeration has the potential to reduce competition. Additionally, it has been argued that financial conglomeration versus separation fosters less innovation. However, Claessens[124] suggests that a separate system can indeed be more innovative in the design of specific financial products, but a conglomerate can be more innovative in the overall production and marketing of financial services.

Anti-competitive market power could, in theory, arise from size alone if barriers to entry are great. It could also evolve through predatory pricing. A large conglomerate could sell at less than the cost of production if it wished to drive out smaller competitors or to discourage new entrants. As a practical matter, this option seems remote, provided there are not substantial barriers to entry. For every large national or multinational financial conglomerate that might attempt such practices, there are several others with the financial capacity to weather the storm. Existing competition law would seem to be sufficient, if enforced reasonably, to

---

[123] S. Claessens, *Benefits and Costs of Integrated Financial Services Provision in Developing Countries.* University of Amsterdam and CEPR, 14 November 2002, pp. 20–21, 25.

[124] S. Claessens, *Benefits and Costs of Integrated Financial Services Provision in Developing Countries.* University of Amsterdam and CEPR, 14 November 2002, p. 30.

prohibit or punish concerted anti-competitive behaviour by conglomerates.[125]

Unregulated entities

The issue of unregulated entities (i.e. entities not subject to oversight by any sector regulator) is relatively important in both cases of regulatory arbitrage. Excessive leveraging can occur when an unregulated parent issues debt or other instruments not acceptable as regulatory capital in a downstream entity and down streams the proceeds to a subsidiary firm in the form of equity or other regulatory capital.[126] While excess leverage from down streaming the proceeds of a parent debt issue is not seen as inherently unsafe and unsound, the parent's obligations can in these circumstances result in undue stress on the regulated subsidiary, particularly where the top-level holding company is itself unregulated.[127] Unregulated intermediate holding companies with financial dependents and affiliates may also facilitate excessive gearing, and thus should be treated as if consolidated in the relevant sector.[128]

With an unregulated holding company, an assessment of group-wide capital adequacy should encompass the effect of the holding company's structure. Regulators will need to be able to obtain information about the holding company's ability to service all external debt. The group-wide capital assessment should eliminate the effect of intermediate holding companies that are typically non-trading entities, whose only assets are their investments in subsidiaries or that provide services to other companies. Finally, some unregulated group entities conduct activities similar to those of regulated companies (e.g., leasing and factoring). In such in-

---

[125] H. D. Skipper Jr., *Financial Services Worldwide: Promises and Pitfalls.* Georgia State University, 2000, pp. 47–48. Available:

http://www.worldbank.org/wbi/banking/insurance/contractual/pdf/skipper.pdf

[126] H. D. Skipper Jr., *Financial Services Worldwide: Promises and Pitfalls.* Georgia State University, 2000, pp. 44–46. Available:

http://www.worldbank.org/wbi/banking/insurance/contractual/pdf/skipper.pdf

[127] C. Half, "Evolving Trends in the Supervision of Financial Conglomerates: A Comparative Investigation of Responses to the Challenges of Cross-Sectoral Supervision in the United States, European Union, and United Kingdom." Harvard Law School: International Finance Seminar, 30 April 2002, p. 28.

[128] C. Half, "Evolving Trends in the Supervision of Financial Conglomerates: A Comparative Investigation of Responses to the Challenges of Cross-Sectoral Supervision in the United States, European Union, and United Kingdom." Harvard Law School: International Finance Seminar, 30 April 2002, p. 28.

stances, a comparable or notional capital proxy may be estimated by applying to the unregulated entity the capital requirements of the most analogous regulated industry. Unregulated non-financial entities would normally be excluded from the assessment of the group.[129]

[129] H. D. Skipper Jr., *Financial Services Worldwide: Promises and Pitfalls.* Georgia State University, 2000, pp. 44–46. Available:
http://www.worldbank.org/wbi/banking/insurance/contractual/pdf/skipper.pdf

Chapter 2

Financial Conglomerates in the European Union

2.1. Banking in the European Union: Importance and Insurance Linkages of Largest Banks

The following part of the survey covers the banking sector in EU countries looking at the largest banks/banking groups defined according to their total assets. The five largest banks in each country are ranked according to their total assets; the statistics have been compiled based on annual figures as of the year ending in 2001. The data for individual banks/banking groups are presented on a consolidated basis, unless a bank is a stand-alone entity. Thus, systematic consistency is achieved by using similar basis of ranking for all banks/banking groups. I have included both banks and banking groups in this survey as most of the largest banking groups in the EU comprise of the largest banks and are also treated in official country rankings accordingly.

The largest banks/banking groups are presented in Table 1. The banks and banking groups in this survey are defined in the meaning of ordinary banking business. The ranking includes all banks, except those that are special purpose banks (e.g., public finance or project finance only) and whose activities do not include any universal banking activities. In different countries, the banking systems differ widely. I have examined commercial banks, local savings banks, co-operative banks, mortgage banks and other credit institutions engaged in universal banking business. Table 1 suggests that no banking structure prevails in top ranking. In some countries (e.g., Germany, the United Kingdom, Belgium and Luxembourg) the largest banks are mainly commercial banks, while in other

Table 1. Largest Banks and Linked Insurance Undertakings in the EU as of 31 December 2001

Country	Rank	Name Bank/Banking Group	Total Assets (EUR Mio)	Related Insurance Undertaking Name	Country
AT	1	Bank Austria Creditanstalt AG	159 596	Victoria Volksbank Versicherungsa.g.	AT
AT	2	Erste Bank der Oesterr. Spark. AG	86 033	Sparkassen Versicherung AG	AT
AT	3	Raiffeisen Zentralbank Oesterr. AG	44 583	Uniqa Versicherungen AG	AT
AT	4	Bank für Arbeit und Wirtschaft AG	39 712	BAWAG Versicherung AG	AT
AT	5	Oesterreichische Postsparkasse AG	11 982	BAWAG Versicherung AG	AT
BE	1	Fortis Bank	378 000	Fortis	BE
BE	2	Dexia Bank Belgique	222 000	DVV De Volksverz.–Les AP	BE
BE	3	KBC Bank NV	216 000	KBC Insurance NV	BE
BE	4	Bank Brussel Lambert–BBL	160 653	BBL Life	BE
BE	5	Axa Bank Belgium	14 089	Axa Belgium SA	BE
DE	1	Deutsche Bank AG	917 669	DB Vida - Comp.de Seguros y Reas.	ES
DE	2	Bayerische Hypo-und Vereinsbank AG	715 860	ERGO Versicherungsgr. AG	DE
DE	3	Dresdner Bank AG	506 345	Allianz Lebensversicherung	DE
DE	4	Commerzbank AG	500 980	x	x
DE	5	Westdeutsche Landesbank AG	423 218	x	x
DK	1	Danske Bank A/S	184 155	Danica Liv & Pension Livsfors.a.s.	DK
DK	2	Realkredit Danmark A/S	71 690	Danica Liv & Pension Livsfors.a.s.	DK
DK	3	Nykredit A/S	69 386	x	x
DK	4	Nordea Bank Danmark Group A/S	66 986	Tryg Forsikring Livsforsikringss.	DK
DK	5	BRF Kredit A/S	19 370	x	x
ES	1	Santander Central Hispano	355 903	Aseguradora Banesto Com de Segur.	ES
ES	2	Banco Bilbao Vizcaya Argentaria	30 547	BBVA Seguros SA de Seguros y Reas.	ES
ES	3	Caja de Ahorros y Pens. de Barc.	87 504	Caixa de Barcelona Seg. de Vida	ES
ES	4	Caja de Ahorros y Monte de P. de M.	66 559	x	x
ES	5	Banco Español de Crédito SA, Banesto	44 689	Aseguradora Banesto Com. de Segur.	ES

Country	No.	Bank	Value	Insurance company		Country
FI	1	Nordea Bank Finland Plc	215 851	Nordea Life Assurance Finland		FI
FI	2	Sampo Bank Plc	20 812	Varma Sampo Mutual Pension Ins.		FI
FI	3	OKO Bank	12 649	Aurum Life Insurance	x	FI
FI	4	Aktiva Savings Bank Plc	3 331		x	x
FI	5	Alandsbanken Abp	1 813		x	x
FR	1	BNP Paribas	825 288	Natio Vie		FR
FR	2	Credit Agricole CA	563 288	Predica		FR
FR	3	Societe Generale	512 499	Sogecap		FR
FR	4	Groupe Caisse d'Epargne	285 896	Ecureuil Vie		FR
FR	5	Credit Mutuel Centre Est Europe	218 800	Groupe des Assur. du Credit Mutuel		FR
GB	1	Barclays Bank Plc	573 477	Barclays Life Assurance Company Ltd		GB
GB	2	Royal Bank of Scotland PLC	338 825	Royal Scottish Assurance Plc		GB
GB	3	HSBC Bank Plc	327 353	HSBC Life (UK) Ltd		GB
GB	4	Lloyds TSB Bank Plc	315 769	Lloyds TSB General Insurance Ltd		GB
GB	5	Abbey National Plc	303 313	Abbey Life Assurance Company Ltd		GB
GR	1	National Bank of Greece SA	52 648	The Ethniki Hellenic Insurance Co		GR
GR	2	Alpha Bank AE	29 904	Alpha Insurance Company AE	x	GR
GR	3	EFG Eurobank Ergasias SA	19 617		x	x
GR	4	Commercial Bank of Greece	18 143	Phoenix General Insurance Co. SA	x	GR
GR	5	Agricultural Bank of Greece	16 243		x	x
IE	1	Allied Irish Banks Plc	86 327	ARK Life Assurance Company	x	IE
IE	2	Bank of Ireland	81 643		x	x
IE	3	Rabobank Ireland Plc	18 682		x	x
IE	4	Permanent TSB Bank	16 583	Irish Life Plc	x	IE
IE	5	Anglo Irish Bank Corporation	15 720		x	x
IT	1	Banca Intesa Spa	313 220	Compangia di Ass. i Riass. Sulla Vita		IT
IT	2	UniCredito Italiano Spa	208 172	Creditras Vita Spa		IT
IT	3	San Paolo IMI	169 347	San Paolo Vita Spa	x	IT
IT	4	Capitalia Spa	131 415		x	x

		Bank		Insurance undertaking		
IT	5	Banca Monte dei Paschi di Siena Spa	116 768	Montepaschi Vita Spa	IT
LU	1	Deutsche Bank Luxembourg SA	48 885	DB Vida - Comp.de Seguros y Reas.	ES
LU	2	Dexia Banque Intern. a Luxembourg	44 708	DVV De Volksverz. – Les AP	BE
LU	3	HVB Banque Luxembourg SA	40 650	ERGO Versicherungsgr. AG	DE
LU	4	Banque Generale du Luxembourg SA	38 996	ERGO Versicherungsgr. AG	DE
LU	5	BNP Paribas Luxembourg	37 009	Natio Vie	FR
NL	1	ABN Amro Holding NV	597 363	ABN Amro Levensverzekering	NL
NL	2	ING Bank NV	443 356	Nationale Nederl. Levenverz.M	NL
NL	3	Rabobank Nederland	363 619	x	x
NL	4	Fortis Bank Nederland (Holding) NV	80 002	AMEV St. Rotterdam Verz. Groep	NL
NL	5	SNS Bank NV	32 416	SNS - Reaal Groep NV	NL
PT	1	Caixa Geral de Depositos	66 462	Companhia de Seg. Fidelidade	PT
PT	2	Banco Comercial Portugues SA	62 952	x	x
PT	3	Banco Espirito Santo SA	38 523	Companhia de Seg. Tranquilidade Vida	PT
PT	4	Banco Totta & Acores	27 366	Aseguradora Banesto Com. de Segur.	ES
PT	5	Banco BPI SA	24 791	BPI Vida - Comp. de Seguros de Vida	PT
SE	1	Svenska Handelsbanken	124 841	SPP Livforsakring AB	SE
SE	2	Skandinaviska Enskilda Banken AB	118 650	SEB Trygg Liv	SE
SE	3	Foereningssparbanken–Swedbank	99 196	Sparebank 1 Skadeforsikring AS	NO
SE	4	Nordea Bank Sweden AB	66 384	Nordea Life Assurance Sweden I, II	SE
SE	5	Stadshypotek AB	38 815	SPP Livforsakring AB	SE

Sources: Bankscope, LexisNexis, annual reports and web pages of Listed banks, insurance undertakings and banking associations

countries with more specific banking structure, there are savings banks and co-operative banks among the largest banks (e.g., France and Italy).

For each ranked bank/banking group I have defined the most important related insurance firms either in the same country or in some other country, if any. Mostly, the ranked banks of the countries are also related to significant insurance business in their countries (e.g., Belgium, the United Kingdom, the Netherlands and Sweden). A few large banks (e.g. Deutsche Bank AG[1] and Banco Totta & Acores) have insurance linkages in other EU countries, while one—the Swedish Foereningssparbanken-Swedbank—has major insurance business only outside the EU, in Norway. Luxembourg presents an exceptional case among the EU countries since all the large banks in the ranking have insurance linkages outside Luxembourg. The situation can be apparently explained by the fact that all the largest banks in Luxembourg are linked to the largest banks of other EU countries and thus reflect the extensive network of bank consolidation in the EU. Most of the banks/banking groups covered by this survey engage in insurance business via subsidiaries, either insurance companies or other specialist operators.

As evidenced by the data of Table 2, all of the five largest German banks are represented among the first twenty banks and banking groups. The largest banks of other large countries, such as France and the United Kingdom, also have an important presence in the ranking. The presence of three large Dutch banks and the Belgian Fortis Bank in the top twenty ranking reflects the well-developed and efficient banking sectors of those small countries.

In addition to previous rankings, there are another five banks and groups that should be considered relevant in order to determine the most important banking-insurance groups. Although their banking activities do not rank among the five largest in their countries, the five institutions are relevant for the survey since they all have insurance linkages and their total assets are quite significant in comparison to other ranked institutions.

---

[1] The figures reflect the situation as of the end of 2001. At the time this book is being prepared, Deutsche Bank AG has realized (and brought to an end) most of its insurance business in all its former locations and has focused mainly on banking and investment activities.

Table 2. Key Figures of the Largest Banks and Banking Groups as of 31 December 2001

	Country	Bank/Banking Group	Total assets (EUR Mio)	Total income (EUR Mio)
1	DE	Deutsche Bank AG	917 669	26 503
2	FR	BNP Paribas	825 288	17 678
3	DE	Bayerische Hypo-und Vereinsbank AG	715 860	10 795
4	NL	ABN Amro Holding NV	597 363	18 834
5	GB	Barclays Bank Plc	573 477	18 597
6	FR	Credit Agricole CA	563 288	7 018
7	FR	Societe Generale	512 499	13 856
8	DE	Dresdner Bank AG	506 345	9 456
9	DE	Commerzbank AG	500 980	7 021
10	NL	ING Bank NV	443 356	4 821
11	DE	Westdeutsche Landesbank AG	423 218	4 535
12	BE	Fortis Bank	378 000	10 042
13	NL	Rabobank Nederland	363 619	7 825
14	ES	Santander Central Hispano	355 903	15 854
15	GB	Royal Bank of Scotland PLC	338 825	22 325*
16	GB	HSBC Bank Plc	327 353	29 438*
17	GB	Lloyds TSB Bank Plc	315 769	14 202*
18	IT	Banca Intesa Spa	313 220	928**
19	ES	Banco Bilbao Vizcaya Argentaria	305 470	13 458
20	GB	Abbey National Plc	303 313	6 943*
		TOTAL	**9 580 815**	**186 293**

* Figures presented reflect the group figures for The Royal Bank of Scotland Group, HSBC Holdings, Lloyds TSB Group and Abbey National Group as of 31 December 2001

** Figures reflect the income statement of Gruppo IntesaBci as of 31 December 2001

Sources: Bankscope, LexisNexis, annual reports and web pages of listed banks

Presented on group basis, the additional insurance linked banks/banking groups are:

1) HBOS Plc of the United Kingdom, with total group assets of EUR 452,026 million;

2) DZ Bank AG-Deutsche Zentral-Genossenschaftsbank of Germany, with total group assets of EUR 358,760 million;

3) Crédit Lyonnais of France, with total group assets of EUR 202,365 million;

4) Groupe Banques Populaires of France, with total group assets of EUR 193,608 million; and

5) Banca Nazionale del Lavoro SA-BNL of Italy, with total assets of EUR 91,388 million.[2]

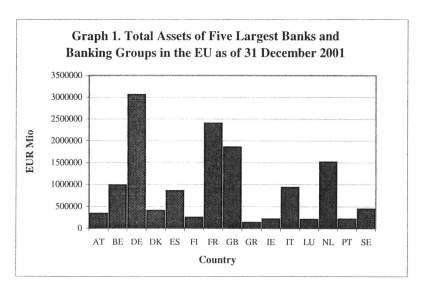

Graph 1. Total Assets of Five Largest Banks and Banking Groups in the EU as of 31 December 2001

Sources: Bankscope, LexisNexis, annual reports and web pages of banks, own calculations

Graph 1 illustrates the aggregated total assets of the five largest banks and banking groups in each country. The figures provided in Graph 1 are given on a consolidated basis[3] and derived from my study on individual institutions. The examination shows that the ratio of total assets of institutions in large countries (e.g., Germany, France and the United Kingdom) is expectedly very high compared to the institutions in smaller countries. In general, the results reflect that the size of the banking market is related to the size of the country. The Netherlands and Belgium—small countries with very well developed banking sector—present an interesting difference from this rule. The Netherlands and Belgium, with the aggregated total assets of their five largest banks and banking groups of EUR 1,516,756 and 990,742 million respectively, stand close to large and medium sized EU countries.

---

[2] Mediobanca R&S. Largest European Banks: Financial Aggregates, 2002. Available: http://www.mbres.it. Some key figures are provided by Bankscope.

[3] In the survey I have used consolidated figures mainly due to the fact that unconsolidated figures were often not accessible.

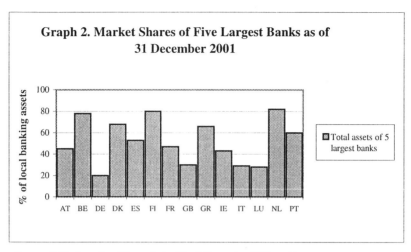

Graph 2. Market Shares of Five Largest Banks as of
31 December 2001

Source: ECB. Occasional Paper Series No. 6, December 2002, p. 42

The comparison between institution-level total assets and total assets of a particular banking sector[4] as a whole reflects the market shares of the five largest banks in each country. In completion of Graph 2 I have used the aggregated data provided by the European Central Bank.[5] The data in Graph 2 suggest that there are significant differences across countries relating to the share of domestic banking assets controlled by the five major banks. Smaller countries like Belgium, Finland and the Netherlands show figures of around 80%, followed by Greece and Portugal with figures about 60%, while Germany has the most dispersed banking system, in which the five largest banks control only 20% of all banking assets. In general, the analysis allows the conclusion that the largest banks and banking groups present a significant market power at the level of their home countries. The finding also indicates that in addition to local impact, the activities of the largest banks and banking groups might have quite a strong common impact on the financial developments of other EU member states. On the other hand, the findings in Table 2 suggest that a relatively large part of the assets of important institutions in the EU bank-

---

[4] According to the European Central Bank, the total assets of the banking sector of the EU amounted to 24 458 778 million euro as of the at the end of 2001 (European Central Bank, EU Banking Sector Stability, February 2003, p. 20).

[5] No figures on Swedish institutions were available in the study of the European Central Bank.

ing sector is concentrated in just a few countries and their extremely large institutions—the "big players."

In the following I will examine the growth and structure of some important "players." Although the banking-insurance relations will be viewed in more detail in the last part of this chapter, I will also highlight some important insurance linkages related to the structure of the banks. Bank concentration and growth of the large institutions in the EU have resulted from significant M&A activities. Between 1 January 1996 and 31 December 2001, 18 "mega-mergers" between EU banks took place; most of the banks involved were of the same national affiliation. Table 3 provides an overview of the largest bank-to-bank intra-EU M&A deals in the years 1996–2001.

In Germany, the merger between Bayerische Vereinsbank and Bayerische Hypotheken-und-Wechsel-Bank in 1998 led to the setting up of Bayerische Hypo- und Vereinsbank (HVB), the second largest bank in Germany (see Table 1). HVB acquired Bank Austria in 2000; the latter had merged with Creditanstalt in 1997. HVB's largest shareholder is the world's largest reinsurer Munich Re, with a stake of 25,6 %. The creation of insurance linkages of another large German bank—Dresdner Bank— relates to the year 2001[6] when one of the largest German insurers— Allianz AG—took control of the bank. German DZ Bank AG functions as a central bank[7] to over 80 % of local co-operative banks. In September 2001, the two German central banks for co-operative banks—DG Bank and GZ-Bank—merged,[8] the name of the bank was changed to DZ Bank.[9] The fifth largest German bank, Westdeutsche Landesbank is a state-controlled company.

In France, Crédit Agricole acquired Banque Indosuez in 1996, while in 1998 the fifth largest bank in the ranking of Table 1—Credit Mutuel— took a majority stake in Union Européenne de CIC as part of its privatization scheme. The second largest banking group, Credit Agricole group, has an inverse pyramidal structure, with the local co-operative banks at the top and Credit Agricole SA acting as a central bank. In 1999, Banque Nationale de Paris acquired Paribas (after having staved off the bid from

---

[6] Allianz AG-Dresdner Bank transaction is not reflected in Table 3.

[7] Central bank of a cooperative bank is a coordinating body. The term does not mean a central bank as a monetary policy institution.

[8] Table 3 does not reflect the DG Bank and DZ-Bank merger.

[9] Mediobanca R&S. Largest European Banks: Financial Aggregates, 2002, pp. 5–6. Available: http://www.mbres.it.

Table 3. Largest Banking Sector M&A Deals in the EU

		Combined Entity			Banks Involved		
	Year	Name	Country	Total Assets* (EUR Mio)	Name	Country	Total Assets* (EUR Mio)
1	1996	Credit Agricole	FR	369 797	Credit Agricole	FR	301 552
					Banque Indosuez	FR	68 245
2	1997	Bank Austria	AT	106 432	Bank Austria	AT	55 799
					Creditanstalt	AT	50 633
3	1998	Bayerische Hypo- und Vereinsbank	DE	411 316	Bayerische Vereinsbank	DE	277 260
					Bayerische Hypotheken- und Wechsel-Bank	DE	184 056
4	1998	ING Groep	NL	379 888	ING Groep	NL	278 505
					Banque Bruxelles Lambert	BE	101 383
5	1998	Fortis	BE	298 579	Fortis	BE	151 392
					Generale de Banque	BE	147 187
6	1998	Landesbank Baden-Württemberg	DE	210 472	Südwestdeutsche Landesbank	DE	116 498
					Landeskreditbank Baden-Württemberg	DE	53 339
					Landesgirokasse	DE	40 635
7	1998	Credit Mutuel	FR	193 819	Credit Mutuel	FR	98 139
					Union Europeenne de CIC	FR	95 680
8	1998	Nordic Baltic Holding Group	SE	97 332	Merita	FI	49 875
					Nordbanken	SE	47 457
9	1999	BNP Paribas	FR	589 941	Banque Nationale de Paris	FR	324 826
					Paribas	FR	265 115
10	1999	IntesaBci	IT	265 933	Banca Intesa	IT	153 077
					Banca Commerciale Italiana	IT	112 856

No.	Year	Name		Total assets	Constituents		Assets*
11	1999	Banco Santander Central Hispano	ES	235 732	Banco Santander Central Hispano	ES	154 161
					Banco Central Hispanoamericano	ES	81 571
12	2000	Bayerische Hypo- und Vereinsbank	DE	643 084	Bayerische Hypo- und Vereinsbank	DE	503 255
					Bank Austria	AT	139 829
13	2000	HSBC Holdings	GB	635 959	HSBC Holdings	GB	566 667
					Credit Commercial de France	FR	69 292
14	2000	The Royal Bank od Scotland Group	GB	441 654	The Royal Bank of Scotland Group	GB	142 918
					National Westminster Bank	GB	298 736
15	2000	Banco Bilbao Vizcaya Argentaria	ES	235 571	Banco Bilbao Vizcaya	ES	154 504
					Argentaria	ES	81 067
16	2000	Nordea	SE	181 240	Nordic Baltic Holding	SE	103 977
					Unidanmark	DK	77 263
17	2000	Danske Bank	DK	168 677	Danske Bank	DK	94 202
					RealDanmark	DK	74 475
18	2001	HBOS	GB	430 423	Halifax Group	GB	292 444
					Bank of Scotland	GB	137 979

* Figures show total assetsin previous year

Source: Mediobanca R&S. Largest European Banks: *Financial Aggregates*, 2002, pp. 8–9. Available: *http://www.mbres.it*

Société Générale) and changed its name to BNP Paribas, which is today the largest banking group in France. In 2000, Crédit Commercial de France was acquired by UK-based concern HSBC Holdings.

Table 3 suggests that in the Benelux countries Banque Bruxelles Lambert was snapped up by the Dutch ING Group in 1998, while in the same year Fortis[10] acquired the largest bank in Belgium—Générale de Banque. Other major same-country transactions include Banco Santander Central Hispano of Spain acquisition of Banco Hispanoamericano in 1999 and Banco Bilbao Vizcaya acquisition of Argentaria in 2000. In fact, Banco Santander Central Hispano seems to have established strategic alliances with the institutions in neighbouring countries in order to gain better results and growth: in 2000 commercial alliance with French Société Générale and transnational collaboration agreement with Italian San Paolo-IMI were conducted.[11] The largest Italian bank, Banca Intesa bought Banca Commerciale Italiana in 1999, while in the United Kingdom the Royal Bank of Scotland bought the National Westminster bank in 2000. In 2001, UK-based group Halifax and the Bank of Scotland formed a single holding company HBOS.

As evidenced, the largest banks in the EU have grown significantly mostly due to M&A transactions. The largest transactions have been mainly between the entities belonging to the same nationality. The structure of the largest banks in a country depends on the traditions and trait of character of the banking sector (e.g., large co-operative banks in France reflect the community orientation of France). Thus, there is no unique formula for the structure of banks in the EU. Commercial banks, savings banks and co-operative banks have proved to be equally efficient in terms of growth. Additionally, the evidence of Table 1 suggests that they have been equally active in establishment of insurance connections.

---

[10] Fortis was, until the end of 2001, shared by two holding companies—the Belgian Fortis S.A. and the Dutch Fortis N.V. In December 2001, the shares of the two holdings were replaced with a single set of shares. The headquarters of Fortis and the centre of its activities are located in Belgium, thus Fortis is formally considered a Belgian group.

[11] *E. Sanchez Peinado,* Internationalisation Process of Spanish Banks: a New Stage After the Mergers. University of Valencia, Faculty of Economics, 2001.

2.2. Insurance in the European Union: Importance and Banking Linkages of Largest Insurance Undertakings

The survey conducted in this part of the chapter covers the insurance sectors in the EU. Similar to the analysis on the banking sector, I have started my survey with defining the largest insurance undertakings according to their total assets. The five largest insurance firms in each country are ranked according to their total assets; the statistics have been compiled on the basis of annual figures as of the year ending in 2001. The data for individual insurance firms are presented on a consolidated basis, unless insurance undertaking is a stand-alone entity.

The list of the largest undertakings is provided in Table 4. I have not distinguished between life and non-life insurance activities in this phase of the survey. For countries with smaller insurance markets, Greece and Portugal, I have defined, accordingly, only two and four of the largest insurance firms, because the rest of the insurance firms in these countries are too small, diversified and do not have an important country-level influence. The insurance firms are ranked as the largest single undertakings in each particular country (usually daughter companies of large groups) and do not reflect the group as a whole. Thus, some of the largest well-known groups (e.g. Allianz, ING, Axa, Generali) are represented in the list but their total group-level influence is not examined in this part of the survey.

For each ranked insurance undertaking I have defined the most important related banking business either in the same country or in some other country, if any. The data suggest that French, German, Belgian and Dutch institutions play important role in insurance business in the EU. In many countries the insurance companies are subsidiaries of previously examined banks/banking groups (e.g., the Predica life insurance company as a subsidiary of French Crédit Agricole and Uniqa Versicherung as a subsidiary of Raiffeisen Zentralbank Österreich AG). In Belgium, the two largest banks—KBC Bank and Fortis Bank—can also be described as major bancassurance groups (ranking accordingly third and first in Belgium) with relatively important insurance activities in their group structure. In both cases, the group structure at its top-level is holding-based. For example, KBC Bank and Insurance Holding is especially designed to perform as an "umbrella" for both banking and insurance businesses.

When it comes to banking and country linkages, the picture looks quite diversified. To a large extent, the ranked insurance firms are also related to banking business in their countries (e.g., German insurers

Table 4. Largest Insurance Undertakings and Linked Banks in the EU as of 31 December 2001

Country	Rank	Name Insurance Undertaking	Total Assets (EUR Mio)	Related Bank/Banking Group Name	Country
AT	1	Uniqa Versicherungen AG	12 452	Raiffeisen Zentralbank Oester. AG	AT
AT	2	Wiener Stadt. Allgemeine Vers.	10 652	x	x
AT	3	Generali Versicherung AG	5 305	Banca Generali Spa - Generbanca	IT
AT	4	Uniqa Personenversicherung	5 049	Raiffeisen Zentralbank Oester. AG	AT
AT	5	Raiffeisen Versicherung AG	4 942	Raiffeisen Zentralbank Oester. AG	AT
BE	1	Fortis	27 789	Fortis Bank	BE
BE	2	AXA Belgium SA	15 259	Axa Bank Belgium	BE
BE	3	KBC Insurance NV	10 395	KBC Bank NV	BE
BE	4	SMAP Societe Mutuelle des A.P	9 886	x	x
BE	5	SMAP Pensions	6 267	x	x
DE	1	ERGO Versicherungsgr. AG	101 439	Bayerische Hypo-und Vereinsbank AG	DE
DE	2	Allianz Lebensversicherung	95 793	Dresdner Bank AG	DE
DE	3	AMB Generali Holdings AG	78 587	Deutsche Bausparkasse Badenia	DE
DE	4	Wuestenrot & Wuertembergis.	53 141	Wuestenrot Bausparkasse AG	DE
DE	5	Gerling Konzern Vers. Beteil. AG	40 323	x	x
DK	1	Danica Liv&Pension Livsfors.	22 554	Danske Bank	DK
DK	2	PFA Pension Forsikrings A/S	20 734	x	x
DK	3	Codan A/S	11 882	x	x
DK	4	Kommunernes Pensionsfors.	8 872	x	x
DK	5	Magistrenes Pensionskasse	5 171	x	x
ES	1	Caifor SA	8 916	Fortis Bank	BE
ES	2	Vida-Caixa SA de Seg. y Reaseg.	8 807	Fortis Bank	BE
ES	3	BBVA Seguros SA de Seg. y Rea.	8 543	Banco Bilbao Vizcaya Argentaria	ES
ES	4	Mapfre Vida SA Seguros y Rea.	8 415	x	x

		Insurance company	Amount	Bank		Country
ES	5	Allianz Comp. de Seguros y Rea.	4 921	Dresdner Bank AG		DE
FI	1	Varma Sampo Mutual Pension In.	16 826	Sampo Bank Plc	x	FI
FI	2	Ilmarinen Mutual Pension Ins.	13 786			x
FI	3	Nordea Life Assurance Finland	6 073	Nordea Bank Finland Plc	x	FI
FI	4	Suomi Mutual Life Assurance Co	5 892		x	x
FI	5	Tapiola Mutual Pension Ins. Co	4 610		x	x
FR	1	CNP Assurances	142 055		x	x
FR	2	AXA	99 584	Axa Banque		FR
FR	3	Predica	83 930	Credit Agricole		FR
FR	4	Groupama	60 056	Banque Finama		FR
FR	5	Ecureuil Vie	51 450	Groupe Caisse d'Epargne	x	FR
GB	1	Legal and General Group Plc	176 569			x
GB	2	Prudential Assurance Co. Ltd	136 222	Prudential Banking Plc*	x	GB
GB	3	Standard Life Assurance Co.	130 387	Standard Life Bank Ltd.		GB
GB	4	CGU International Insurance Plc	128 252	Delta Lloyd Bankengroep NV		NL
GB	5	Royal & Sun Alliance Insurance Plc	100 982		x	x
GR	1	The Ethniki Hellenic Insurance Co	1 250	National Bank of Greece SA		GR
GR	2	Phoenix General Insurance Co.	366	Commercial Bank of Greece		GR
IE	1	Hibernian Life and Pensions Ltd	5 230	Delta Lloyd Bankengroep NV	x	NL
IE	2	Hannover Reinsurance (Ireland)	3 274			x
IE	3	Eagle Star Life Assurance Co	2 510		x	x
IE	4	Scottish Mutual International Plc	1 792	Abbey National Plc	x	GB
IE	5	Allianz Irish Life Holdings Plc	1 508	Dresdner Bank (Ireland) Plc		IE
IT	1	Riunione Adriatica di Sicurta Spa	43 146	Dresdner Bank AG		DE
IT	2	Alleanza Assicurazioni Spa	22 638	Banca Generali Spa - Generbanca		IT
IT	3	INA Vita Spa	19 549	Banca Generali Spa - Generbanca		IT
IT	4	Toro Assicurazioni Spa	18 387		x	x
IT	5	Compagnia Assicuratrice Unipol	16 341	Unipol Banca Spa		IT
LU	1	Lombard International Assurance	2 888			x

LU	2	PanEuro Life SA	x	2 648		x
LU	3	Foyer Compagnie Lux. SA	x	1 751		x
LU	4	Scottish Equitable Intern. SA		1 739	Aegon Bank NV	NL
LU	5	Vitis Life Luxembourg SA		1 130	Kredietbank S.A. Luxembourgeoise	LU
NL	1	Aegon NV		264 061	Aegon Bank NV	NL
NL	2	Nationale Nederl. Levensverz M		55 949	ING Bank N.V.	NL
NL	3	SNS - Reaal Groep NV		43 761	SNS Bank NV	NL
NL	4	Achmea Holding NV		39 876	Achmea Bank Holding NV	NL
NL	5	Delta Lloyd NV		34 239	Delta Lloyd Bankengroep NV	NL
PT	1	Seguros e Pensoes Gere SGPS**		8 283	Achmea Bank Holding NV	PT
PT	2	Companhia de Seg. Tranquilidade		4 282	Banco Espirito Santo SA	PT
PT	3	Companhia de Seg. Fidelidade		3 781	Caixa Geral de Depositos	PT
PT	4	Mundial Confianca Comp. de Seg.		2 790	Caixa Geral de Depositos	PT
SE	1	Skandia Insurance Co. Ltd		64 121	Skandiabanken	SE
SE	2	Alecta Pensionsforsakring Oms.	x	36 962		x
SE	3	Arbetsmarkn. Pensionsförs AB	x	22 841		x
SE	4	Gamla Livförs AB SEB Trygg Liv		18 127	Skandinaviska Enskilda Banken AB	SE
SE	5	Folksam Mutual Life Insurance	x	6 570		x

* In April 2002 the name was changed to EGG Banking
** The undertaking was bought back by Banco Comercial Portugues in 2002
Source: ISIS, Bankscope, LexisNexis, annual reports and web pages of listed insurance firms, banks, insurance associations

ERGO Versicherungsgrupp AG and Allianz Lebensversicherung; Belgian bancassurance businesses; and Nordea group's activities in Finland). On the other hand, some large insurance firms (e.g. CGU International Insurance of the United Kingdom and Austrian Generali Versicherung AG) have bank linkages in other EU countries. The evidence demonstrates a significant presence of German insurer Allianz in other EU countries (e.g., Italy and Spain) and also relative importance of Dutch insurance business (e.g., Aegon NV).

There are some more important findings related to insurance-banking linkages: it is not only banks that act as parent/holding companies for insurers, but the system also functions the other way around. Generali, Allianz, Axa, Prudential Plc, Aegon NV and Achmea Holding are the important insurance companies that have broadened their activities into banking business. In some countries, most of the largest insurance undertakings stay separate from banking (e.g., Denmark, Luxembourg and Sweden) or belong to large insurance groups with no other activities (e.g., SMAP of Belgium, Royal & Sun Alliance of the United Kingdom and French CNP Assurances). In Denmark and Sweden, the situation can be explained by the strong social policy system which has encouraged the establishment of local/community-level pension insurance schemes.

I will now briefly examine life and non-life insurance specialisations of the largest ranked companies. Health insurance is generally considered as non-life insurance. Among the ten largest companies, UK-based Legal & General Group, Royal & Sun Alliance and French CNP Assurances are insurance providers that are not linked to traditional banking business. CNP Assurances is focused mainly on life insurance, while Royal & Sun Alliance has significant activities in the field of non-life business. In relation to the major insurance business countries the findings vary: in the United Kingdom the largest undertakings are strongly specialised either in life-business (e.g., Prudential Assurance[12]) or non-life business (e.g., Royal & Sun Alliance and CGU International Insurance[13]), while in most other countries the largest insurers are involved in both life and non-life business (e.g. German Allianz, French AXA).

In order to determine the importance of ranked insurance firms Graph 3 provides a comparison between the total assets of ranked insurance firms and the EU insurance market in total. The evidence suggests that in

---

[12] Prudential Assurance belongs to Prudential Plc and Standard Life Insurance Plc.

[13] CGU International Insurance belongs to UK-based Aviva Plc group.

terms of assets, the ranked firms (total assets amounting to EUR 2,500,000 million) cover over 50 % of total assets of insurance sector in the EU. This clearly indicates that the largest insurance undertakings play an important role at both domestic and EU level. Another important conclusion can be drawn from the previous analyses: as most of the largest insurance firms are strongly connected to banking in the EU, linked banks are therefore open to insurance-related risks. Because the linkages between banking and insurance are as extensive as the evidence suggests and involve major "players" in both sectors, banking-insurance conglomeration is a serious concern of systemic risk and crisis management at both country level and at the EU level. Additionally, the EU insurance sector has influence on the world insurance market and vice versa.

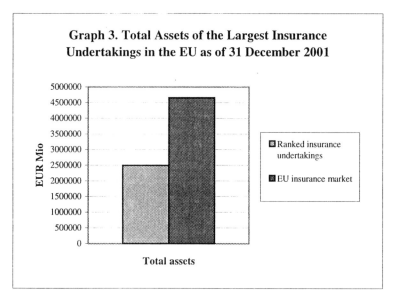

Graph 3. Total Assets of the Largest Insurance Undertakings in the EU as of 31 December 2001

Sources: ISIS, LexisNexis, annual reports and web pages of insurance undertakings, CEA, own calculations

The data given in Graph 4 suggest that EU insurance undertakings play a relatively important role in the world insurance market. The ratio of non-life premiums of the EU insurance undertakings amounts to 27.46% of the world market, while it is expectedly slightly higher for life-insurance—29.99% of the world market. When looking at non-life and life insurance segments in the world, the evidence suggests that in spite of the market share of close to 1/3 of non-life insurance business in the

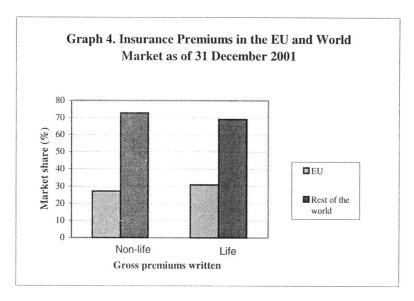

Graph 4. Insurance Premiums in the EU and World Market as of 31 December 2001

Sources: CEA, own calculations

world, the EU insurance sector has less significance at world level in non-life insurance than it has in life insurance business. The reason for this is that the USA holds traditionally strong positions in non-life insurance, having the market share of over 47 % of the world non-life insurance market. Thus, the non-life insurance market of the world is not shared in roughly equal stakes to enable large stakeholders to share the influence but is rather influenced by one "big player." On the contrary, in the life-insurance market of the world, the EU insurance sector holds an important stake together with other large stakeholders—Japan (25%) and the USA (31%). The most important EU insurance country, the United Kingdom (with its largest institutions Prudential Plc., Standard Life Insurance, etc.) alone has close to 11% of the share.[14]

2.3. Major Banking-Insurance Groups in the European Union

This part of the second chapter is to draw conclusions from the previous analyses and examine briefly the most important domestic and intra-EU formations of banking-insurance groups. Most of the previously exam-

[14] Comité Européen des Assurances. European Insurance in Figures, Complete Data 2001.

ined banks and insurance firms are related to other corresponding sectors and thus form parts of banking-insurance groups in the EU. The largest banks are mainly in the centre of groups and conduct their insurance activities in the form of bancassurance.

Bancassurance in its simplest form is the distribution of insurance products through a bank's distribution channels. Bancassurance describes a package of financial services that can fulfil both banking and insurance needs at the same time. By successfully mining their customer databases, leveraging their reputation and distribution systems to make appointments, and utilising sales techniques tailored to the middle market, European banks have increased the insurance leads into sales. The increased sales profitability makes one look at bancassurance as a highly profitable option. Some of the largest bancassurance groups—Lloyds TSB in the UK, Credit Agricole in France and Spain's Banco Bilbao Vizcaya—have delivered outstanding results. These banks have profitably sold insurance products to more than a fourth of their customers while generating more than 20% on sales.[15]

Among leading banking-insurance groups, there are also groups, which are headed by insurance undertakings. Groups such as French AXA, German Allianz, UK-based Prudential Plc and Aviva Plc and Dutch Aegon NV are important in both insurance and banking. Some of them have also contributed quite significantly to the largest banking-insurance M&A transactions in the EU.

The final results on the identification of major banking-insurance groups in the EU in the year ending in 2001 are provided in Table 5. The major groups are ranked according to their total assets on a consolidated basis and the list comprises of the groups engaged in both banking and insurance activities. The list is not conclusive due to the limited scope of research and data availability. Based on the previous study of the largest banks and insurance companies, the list of major banking-insurance groups is consistent with the research scope of the book. Table 5 aims to map the most significant banking-insurance groups in the EU, their most important banking and insurance activities and reflect the significant asset-base of the groups. Table 5 covers all the institutions examined during my survey and found to match the criterion of banking-insurance linkages. I have not separately looked at smaller and less significant institu-

---

[15] M. Kumar, Bancassurance. Financial Express, 11 April 2000. Available: http://www.einsuranceprofessional.com/ artbuzz.htm

tions, but have tried to cover all the important "players" whose activities might have influence at the EU level.

The data suggest that the leading EU countries of banking and insurance industry (e.g., Germany, the United Kingdom, France, Belgium and the Netherlands) are expectedly on the top of the ranking of banking-insurance groups. With Deutsche Bank AG as the only exception, the top 10 ranked groups conduct significant business in both insurance and banking. The structure of listed groups varies and one can draw a conclusion that it depends much on system and practice in different countries. Many of the groups listed in Table 5 are headed by banks (e.g., French BNP Paribas, Crédit Agricole, Société Générale and Italian Banca Intesa), while other bank-initiated groups have preferred holding structures (e.g., UK-based HSBC Holding Plc., Dutch ING Group and Swedish Nordea AB).

Insurance-headed groups mostly tend to have holding structures (e.g., Dutch Aegon and French AXA). Additionally, the evidence suggests that some groups use a holding structure which is not related to a particular bank or insurance undertaking but is rather a formal "umbrella" for those activities. Usually the name of such a holding does not indicate banks/insurance firms collected under this "umbrella" (e.g., Aviva, Almanij, Munich Re Group[16] and Eureko B.V.[17]).

[16] Munich Re Group has a stake of 25,6% in the second largest bank in Germany, Bayerische Hypo- und Vereinsbank AG (HVB). According to its Annual Report 2001, Munich Re Group considers HVB as its equity participation but the accounts of HVB are not consolidated into the group accounts of Munich Re. Thus, from a formal point of view, HVB should not be identified as a part of Munich Re Group, but substantially I have found it extremely important to show the connections between HVB and Munich Re Group. HVB has strong connections with insurance activities of Munich Re Group, which may have important influence on HVB. Additionally, banking databases consider Munich Re as an ultimate shareholder of HVB.

[17] In the frames of insurance cooperation between Eureko B.V. and Banco Comercial Portugues, Eureko B.V. bought an insurance subsidiary of Banco Comercial Portugues, Seguros e Pensoes Gere, in 2001. Thus, at the year-end 2001, Banco Comercial Portugues had no insurance business on its own and could not be classified as bank-insurance group in Table 5. The second largest bank in Portugal, Banco Comercial Portugues SA, is today the second leading bank-insurance group in Portugal, as Seguros and Pensoes Gere was bought back from Eureko B.V. in 2002.

Table 5. Major Banking-Insurance Groups in the EU as of 31 December 2001

	NAME	Country	Total Assets (EUR Mio)	Most important related bank	Country	Most important related insurance firm	Country
1	Deutsche Bank AG*	DE	917 670	Deutsche Bank AG	DE	DB Vida- Comp. de Seg. y Reas.	ES
2	Allianz AG	DE	911 926	Dresdner Bank AG	DE	Allianz Lebensversicherung AG	DE
3	BNP Paribas	FR	825 288	BNP Paribas	FR	Natio Vie	FR
4	HSBC Holdings Plc	GB	778 591	HSBC Bank Plc	GB	HSBC Life (UK) Ltd	GB
5	ING Group-Internationale Nederlanden Groep NV	NL	705 119	ING Bank NV	NL	Nationale Nederl. Lebenvers. M.	NL
6	ABN Amro Holding NV	NL	597 363	ABN Amro Holding NV	NL	ABN Amro Levensverzekering	NL
7	The Royal Bank of Scotland Group Plc	GB	590 034	Royal Bank of Scotland Plc	GB	Royal Scottish Assurance Plc	GB
8	Barclays Plc	GB	573 477	Barclays Bank Plc	GB	Barclays Life Assurance Co Ltd	GB
9	Crédit Agricole CA	FR	563 289	Crédit Agricole CA	FR	Predica	FR
10	Société Générale	FR	512 499	Société Générale	FR	Sogecap	FR
11	Fortis	BE	475 411	Fortis Bank	BE	Fortis	BE
12	AXA	FR	474 000	Axa Banque	FR	AXA	FR
13	HBOS Plc	GB	452 027	Bank of Scotland	GB	Halifax General Insurance	GB
14	DZ Bank AG-Deutsche Zentral-Genossenschaftsbank	DE	358 760	DZ Bank AG-Deutsche Zentral-Genoss.bank	DE	R+V Versicherung	DE
15	Santander Central Hispano	ES	355 904	Santander Central Hispano	ES	Aseguradora Banesto Com.de S.	ES
16	Dexia	BE	351 250	Dexia Bank Belgique	BE	DVV De Volksverz.—Les AP	BE
17	Banca Intesa SpA	IT	313 220	Banca Intesa SpA	IT	Comp.di Ass.i Riass. Sulla Vita	IT
18	Lloyds TSB Group Plc	GB	312 889	Lloyds TSB Bank Plc	GB	Lloyds TSB General Insurance	GB
19	Banco Bilbao Vizcaya Argentaria, S.A.	ES	305 470	Banco Bilbao Vizcaya Argentaria S.A.	ES	BBVA Seguros SA de Seg. y Re.	ES
20	Abbey National Plc	GB	303 313	Abbey National Plc	GB	Abbey Life Assurance Co Ltd	GB
21	Aviva Plc	GB	300 852	Delta Lloyd Bankengroep NV	NL	CGU International Insurance Plc	GB
22	Groupe Caisse d'Epargne	FR	285 896	Groupe Caisse d'Epargne	FR	Ecureuil Vie	FR

23	Aegon NV	NL	264 061	Aegon Bank NV	NL	Aegon NV	NL
24	Almanij	BE	259 302	KBC Bank NV	BE	KBC Insurance NV	BE
25	Prudential Plc	GB	255 846	Prudential Banking Plc	GB	Prudential Assurance Co Ltd	GB
26	Nordea AB	SE	241 549	Nordea Bank Finland Plc	FI	Nordea Life Assurance Finland	FI
27	Generali Assicurazioni SpA	IT	222 936	Banca Generali Spa-Generbanca	IT	Alleanza Assicurazioni SpA	IT
28	Credit Mutuel–CIC	FR	218 801	Credit Mutuel Centre Est Europe	FR	Groupe des Ass.du Credit Mutuel	FR
29	Danske Bank A/S	DK	208 961	Danske Bank A/S	DK	Danica Liv&Pension Linsfors.a.s.	DK
30	UniCredito Italiano SpA	IT	208 172	UniCredito Italiano SpA	IT	Creditras Vita Spa	IT
31	Crédit Lyonnais	FR	202 365	Crédit Lyonnais	FR	Union des Assurances Federales	FR
32	Groupe Banques Populaires	FR	193 608	Groupe Banques Populaires	FR	Natexis Assurances	FR
33	Munich Re Group	DE	190 060	Bayerische Hypo-und Vereinsbank AG	DE	ERGO Versicherungsgr. AG	DE
34	San Paolo IMI	IT	169 347	San Paolo IMI	IT	San Paolo Vita Spa	IT
35	Standard Life Assurance Company	GB	130 387	Standard Life Assurance Company	GB	Standard Life Bank Ltd	GB
36	Svenska Handelsbanken	SE	124 841	Svenska Handelsbanken	SE	SPP Livforsakring AB	SE
37	Skandinaviska Enskilda Banken AB	SE	118 650	Skandinaviska Enskilda Banken AB	SE	SEB Trygg Liv	SE
38	Gruppo Monte dei Paschi di Siena	IT	116 768	Banca Monte dei Paschi di Siena	IT	Montepaschi Vita Spa	IT
39	Foereningssparbanken - Swedbank	SE	99 196	Foereningssparbanken–Swedbank	SE	Sparebank 1 Skadeforsikring AS	NO
40	Banca Nazionale del Lavoro SA - BNL	IT	91 388	Banca Nazionale del Lavoro SA–BNL	IT	BNL Vita	IT
41	Caja de Ahorros y Pens. de Barcelona	ES	87 504	Caja de Ahorros y Pens. de Barcelona	ES	Caixa de Barcelona Seg. De Vida	ES
42	Allied Irish Banks plc	IE	86 328	Allied Irish Banks plc	IE	ARK Life Assurance Company	IE
43	Erste Bank	AT	86 033	Erste Bank der Oesterr. Sparkassen	AT	Sparkassen Versicherung AG	AT
44	Caixa Geral de Depositos	PT	66 462	Caixa Geral de Depositos	PT	Companhia de Seg. Fidelidade	PT
45	Skandia Insurance Company Ltd.	SE	64 121	Skandiabanken	SE	Skandia Insurance Company Ltd.	SE
46	Groupama	FR	60 056	Banque Finama	FR	Groupama	FR

No.	Name		Value	Bank		Insurance	
47	Eureko B.V.	NL	53 204	Achmea Bank Holding NV	NL	Achmea Holding NV	NL
48	Wuestenrot & Wuertembergisse AG	DE	53 141	Wuestenrot Bausparkasse AG	DE	Wuestenrot & Wuertembergisse AG	DE
49	National Bank of Greece SA	GR	52 648	National Bank of Greece SA	GR	The Ethniki Hellenic Insurance Co.	GR
50	BAWAG PSK Group	AT	47 942	Bank für Arbeit und Wirtschaft AG	AT	BAWAG Versicherung AG	AT
51	Raiffeisen Zentralbank Oesterreich AG	AT	44 584	Raiffeisen Zentralbank Oesterreich AG	AT	Uniqa Versicherungen AG	AT
52	SNS Reaal Groep	NL	43 761	SNS Bank NV	NL	SNS Reaal Groep	NL
53	Espirito Santo Financial Group S.A.	LU	42 748	Banco Espirito Santo SA	PT	Companhia de Seg.Tranquilidade Vida	PT
54	Irish Life & Permanent Plc	IE	34 407	Permanent TSB Bank	IE	Irish Life Plc	IE
55	Alpha Bank AE	GR	30 684	Alpha Bank AE	GR	Alpha Insurance Company AE	GR
56	Okobank Group	FI	30 031	OKO Bank	FI	Aurum Life Insurance	FI
57	Sampo Plc	FI	29 400	Sampo Bank Plc	FI	Varma Sampo Mutual Pension Ins.	FI
58	Banco BPI SA	PT	24 791	Banco BPI SA	PT	BPI Vida–Comp.de Seguros de Vida	PT
59	Commercial Bank of Greece	GR	18 143	Commercial Bank of Greece	GR	Phoenix General Insurance Co. SA	GR
60	Compagnia Assicuratrice Unipol SpA	IT	16 341	Unipol Banca Spa	IT	Compagnia Assicuratrice Unipol SpA	IT

* In 1992 a majority stake in Deutscher Herold insurance was taken by Deutsche Bank AG. The stake was realised later, today Deutscher Herold belongs to Zürich Gruppe and performs as an insurance partner for Deutsche Bank AG.

Source: Bankscope, ISIS, LexisNexis, annual reports and web pages of listed banks, insurance undertakings, banking and insurance associations

In order to support my previous analyses and to understand the formation and rise of some of the largest financial conglomerates, I have examined the latest major banking-insurance M&A activities. I have observed both domestic and intra-EU deals. I have looked at the deals from 1990 to 2001 and listed them into two categories—the ones initiated by a credit institution and those initiated by an insurance undertaking. Reflecting the most important cross-sector conglomeration deals in the EU, Table 6 covers only the largest deals according to deal values and does not seek to look at the size of the stake acquired.

The data suggest that the country coverage of cross-sector M&A activities is similar to earlier examined M&A activities in the EU banking sector: the most important deals (e.g., Lloyds TSB Group's acquisition of Scottish Widows Fund & Life, Allianz AG's acquisition of Dresdner Bank AG) have been domestic deals, i.e. between the entities with the same country of origin. At first glance the examination of total deal values leads to the conclusion that contradicts previous research results indicating at banks as the initiators and centre of banking-insurance groups. Indeed, the numerical evidence of cross-sector deal values in Table 6 allows the conclusion that insurance undertakings have been more active and important in both domestic and cross-border formation of groups.

However, the previous conclusion is misleading as only a few large deals contribute significantly to the overall deal values on behalf of insurance acquirers (e.g., Allianz AG—Dresdner Bank, Fortis-Generale de Banque, ING Groep—BBL and BHF Bank deals), while the average deal values are more stable in the case of bank acquirers. The average deal values, on the contrary, bring one to the conclusion that domestic deals with a bank as an acquirer and insurance firm as a target are the dominant form of M&A activities.

A distinguishing feature in the EU is the relative importance of domestic, cross-industry acquisitions of insurance firms. The data support the finding provided in the first chapter of the book—financial conglomeration has increased remarkably during the last years. About 65 % of all the ranked M&A transactions were completed between 1999 and 2001. The United Kingdom and Belgium dominated in the largest bank-initiated deals while a significant part of the contribution to the insurer-initiated deals fell mainly to smaller countries—the Netherlands and Belgium. In both countries, relatively few, albeit very large, acquisitions enabled conglomerates pairing banking concerns with insurance companies ("bancassurance") to emerge.

Table 6. Largest M&A Deals between EU Banks and Insurance Undertakings in 1990–2001

BANK ▶ INSURANCE UNDERTAKING
DOMESTIC AND INTRA-EU DEALS

	Acquirer	Country	Target	Country	Deal Value (EUR Mio)	Year of Completion
1	Lloyds TSB Group Plc	GB	Scottish Widows Fund & Life	GB	11 950 027	2000
2	Abbey National Plc	GB	Scottish Provident Institution	GB	2 937 842	2001
3	Irish Permanent Plc	IE	Irish Life Plc	IE	2 720 613	1999
4	Lloyds TSB Group Plc	GB	Lloyds Abbey Life Plc	GB	2 079 410	1996
5	Wuestenrot Beteiligungs GmbH	DE	Wuerttembergische AG Versicherung	DE	2 067 178	1999
6	Skandinaviska Enskilda Banken	SE	Trygg-Hansa AB	SE	2 005 423	1997
7	Banco Santander Central Hispano	ES	Cia de Seguros Mundial	PT	1 671 755	2000
8	Halifax Group Plc	GB	Equitable Life Assurance Society	GB	1 666 175	2001
9	Caixa Geral de Depositos SA	PT	Cia de Seguros Mundial	PT	1 405 163	2000
10	Unidanmark A/S	DK	Tryg-Baltica Forsikring	DK	1 208 560	1999
				TOTAL	29 712 146	

INSURANCE UNDERTAKING ▶ BANK
DOMESTIC AND INTRA-EU DEALS

	Acquirer	Country	Target	Country	Deal Value (EUR Mio)	Year of Completion
1	Allianz AG	DE	Dresdner Bank AG	DE	22 303 350	2001
2	Fortis AG	BE	Generale de Banque SA	BE	10 494 526	1998
3	Nationale Nederlanden NV	NL	NMB Postbank Groep NV	NL	5 561 439	1991
4	ING Groep NV	NL	BBL	BE	4 108 796	1997
5	ING Groep NV	NL	BHF Bank	DE	2 326 967	1999
6	Fortis (NL) NV	NL	Banque Generale du Luxembourg	LU	1 750 351	2000
7	Vakuutusosakeyhtio Sampo	FI	Leonia Bank PLC	FI	1 665 149	2000
8	Fortis International NV	NL	ASLK-CGER Banque (Belgium)	BE	1 515 862	1999
9	Fortis SA	BE	MeesPierson NV (ABN-AMRO Hldg)	NL	1 306 524	1997
10	ING Groep NV	NL	BHF Bank	DE	1 257 360	1998
				TOTAL	52 290 324	

Sources: Mergerstat, SDC Platinum, annual reports and web pages of listed banks and insurance undertakings

The average size of deals suggests that the more recent transactions involving larger banks have typically been more ambitious and aim to enhance competitive positions in more integrated markets. There is no doubt that EU banking is profitable and therefore there are necessary capital resources available for the financing of M&A activities. One can conclude that the M&A wave has had substantial implications for owner-ship structures, market concentration and capacity utilisation.

It is often argued that only cross-border M&A activities are relevant for integration. This is not unambiguously the case since domestic M&As too have been motivated by a desire to strengthen market positions with a view to competing effectively in the area-wide dimension. In several EU countries there has been at least one large transaction that led to the crea-tion of a dominant domestic institution (e.g., Bayerische HypoVereins-bank in Germany). The domestic intra-sector and cross-sector transaction activities took place in the United Kingdom. This finding is consistent with the casual observation that the increased integration of European financial and capital markets prompted many UK (and non-UK) financial institutions to seek a foothold in London or expand their existing opera-tions in that financial centre. The increase in the average size of transac-tions after 1999 indicates that acquirers are concerned with becoming large players and they seem to strongly favour the benefits of synergies. The costs of maintaining close proximity to retail customers may be spread over an increasing range of retail products that create economies of scope (e.g., between traditional banking, asset management and insur-ance products).

When it comes to the significance of banking-insurance groups, the asset-base of the groups is remarkable. As I was not able to obtain any market data on total banking-insurance aggregated assets for the EU and/or the world there are no comparisons available between the listed banking-insurance groups and overall banking-insurance activities of the EU/rest of the world. However, when looking at the previous compara-tive analyses on the significance of the single largest banks and insurance firms, one can conclude that similar reasoning applies to the groups in-volved. Taking into consideration the previous analyses and the asset-base in general (and without looking at the required thresholds[18]), most of

---

[18] EU legislation provides for the financial thresholds that determine whether the group is considered for the application of additional supervision criteria of financial con-glomerates

the listed groups can (and evidently will) be considered important "players" in the financial services provision both at their domestic and the EU-level. Thus, most of the defined banking-insurance groups will probably become subject to the supplementary supervision regime of financial conglomerates.

Chapter 3

Financial Conglomerates of the European Union in the New Member States

3.1. Banking and Insurance Sectors in the New Member States

This chapter seeks to determine linkages between previously defined EU banking-insurance groups and the banking/insurance sector in the new member states. The starting point of my analysis is to provide an overview of banking and financial sectors in the new member states and to determine country-specific factors related to the rationale of financial consolidation across the new member states. With the 10 new member states—Cyprus, the Czech Republic, Estonia, Hungary, Latvia, Lithuania, Malta, Poland, Slovakia and Slovenia—the Accession Treaty was signed on 16 April 2003[1] and they joined the EU on 1 May 2004.

The largest new member states are the Czech Republic, Hungary and Poland. Poland has the largest financial sector among the new member states. Slovenia and the Slovak Republic are smaller, but have in many aspects a relatively similar degree of development. The three Baltic States—Estonia, Latvia and Lithuania—are strongly inter-linked amongst themselves with regard to their banking sectors, although their orientation and institutional arrangements are significantly different. Among all the new member states Malta and Cyprus remain slightly on their own as they are not transition economies, but have established market economies that are integrated into the global system. The structure of the banking and financial sectors of the new member states is presented in Table 7.

---

[1] European Commission, Enlargement Directorate-General. *Enlargement of the European Union: An Historic Opportunity,* Brussels, May 2003.

Table 7. Structure of Banking and Insurance Sectors in the New Member States as of 31 December 2001

COUNTRY	Banks					Insurance Undertakings	
	Total Number of Commercial Banks	Number of Foreign Owned Commercial Banks	Foreign Owned Share in Total Banking Assets (%)	State Owned Share in Total Banking Assets (%)	Share in Financial Sector Total Assets (%)	Total Number	Share in Financial Sector Total Assets (%)
Cyprus*	9	NA	NA	NA	NA	NA	NA
Czech Republic	38	26	95	3.8	81.1	43	5.9
Estonia	7	4	96	0	NA	14	NA
Hungary	41	31	76	9	86.3	22	7.2
Latvia	23	10	68	3.2	NA	21	NA
Lithuania	14	4	88	12.2	NA	31	NA
Malta*	16	NA	NA	NA	NA	18	NA
Poland	64	46	70	24.4	84.9	71	8.4
Slovakia	19	12	90	4.9	92.7	28	6.6
Slovenia	24	5	16	48.4	88	15	NA

* Due to the specific of the financial system and limited data availability, most of the figures on Cyprus and Malta are not presented

Source: European Commission, European Economy. Enlargement Papers, November 2002; national central banks and supervisory authorities

Table 7 reflects the dominant role of commercial banks in financial intermediation. The available data suggest that the core of the financial sector—banking—accounts for over 80% of the total assets in the financial system. Although Poland, Hungary, the Czech Republic, Slovakia and Slovenia show similarly high bank dominance, the countries' banking sectors greatly differ. The financial system of Poland is dominated by banks, which are also leaders of larger financial groups. The largest bank, however, is still not privatised. The banking sector in Poland is highly concentrated and in the last years M&As have been often initiated by foreign owners that merge in-a-country business after the mergers of their parent companies abroad.[2] The Czech financial sector is relatively large and the banking sector comprises of mainly typical universal banking. Within the Slovenian banking sector, as well, the most important institutions are typical universal banks, while the Hungarian financial sector is slightly more varied (as non-bank financial intermediaries are rapidly gaining ground). Still, in Hungary, credit institutions perform the vast bulk of financial intermediation and non-bank financial intermediation is not independent of banks' activities. For the Slovak banking sector, the most important event in 2001 was the accomplishment of restructuring and the privatisation of major banks which has led to a highly capitalised and liquid banking market at present.[3]

The banking sector of the new member states is rather concentrated and in most countries (except Slovenia) the foreign share of banking assets is close to 80 %. Table 7 indicates that the state and foreign investors control almost the entire banking sector in most new member states. Commercial banks are mostly privately held and frequently with foreign shareholding. However, some figures (the number of banks, state shareholding and the number of insurance firms) in countries of similar size (e.g., the Baltic States) vary largely. This indicates that there are country-specific factors other than size and location which often determine the developments of the financial sector. For example, Estonia's banking sector is the most developed one among all the new member states while

[2] L. Balcerowicz, "Towards Integration: Evolution of the Financial System of Accession Countries and their Integration with the EU Financial System. Centre for Financial Studies, Colloquium: Globalisation of Financial Markets—Risks and Opportunities." Frankfurt am Main, March 2003.

[3] Czech National Bank, National Bank of Hungary, National Bank of Poland, National Bank of Slovakia, Bank of Slovenia. *Stability and Structure of Financial Systems in CEC5*. Warsaw, May 2002, pp. 9–27, 34–46.

other Baltic states are less advanced. Additionally, Estonia represents the case of excessive foreign ownership in banking and it is the only accession country with a wholly privatised banking sector.[4]

When it comes to the insurance sector, Table 7 suggests that competition from insurance business is only gradually building up. Insurance companies tend to be small in terms of assets and influence. In the countries examined the insurance sector is the second largest segment in the financial system. However, in Slovakia and Slovenia the insurance sectors have little country level importance. Among the three largest countries, the Polish insurance sector has the strongest growth potential for this segment (e.g., life insurance is still relatively underdeveloped). All segments of the Czech financial sector have undergone a process of extensive consolidation. Although the role of insurance is relatively underdeveloped by international comparison, the Czech insurance market is strongly competitive. Life and non-life insurance is not yet separated, but all insurance companies will be transformed into life or non-life companies by 2010. In Hungary bancassurance has been gaining more and more ground. In addition to contractual co-operation, an increasing number of insurance companies are backed by banks as owners.[5]

3.2. Presence and Importance of the European Union Banking-Insurance Groups in the New Member States

Similar to the previous study on the EU banks and insurance firms, this survey covers the five largest banks and insurance undertakings in each new member state. Banking institutions are ranked according to their total assets as of the year ending in 2001 while the basis for the assessment of insurance businesses is gross written premiums. Aggregated sector data in comparison with the data of individual institutions and EU-relations are used to draw conclusions on the significance and EU-linkages of the largest institutions in the new member states.

---

[4] L. Balcerowicz, "Towards Integration: Evolution of the Financial System of Accession Countries and their Integration with the EU Financial System. Centre for Financial Studies, Colloquium: Globalisation of Financial Markets—Risks and Opportunities." Frankfurt am Main, March 2003.

[5] Czech National Bank, National Bank of Hungary, National Bank of Poland, National Bank of Slovakia, Bank of Slovenia. *Stability and Structure of Financial Systems in CEC5*. Warsaw, May 2002, pp. 9–27.

3.2.1. Largest Banks in the New Member States and the European Union Linkages

Table 8 presents the five largest banks and banking groups, also indicating whether they are ultimately controlled by domestic or foreign shareholders and showing the linkages with the EU banking-insurance groups. For the largest banking sectors among the new member states—Poland, Hungary and the Czech Republic—the data suggest that the first of the largest banks in Poland and Hungary are controlled by domestic capital, accounting for 18.9% and 24.1% respectively of assets of the banking market in total. Both countries reflect the former trend of extensive state-ownership in banking. The Hungarian largest, National Savings and Commercial Bank—OTP Bank—was a state-owned bank for a relatively long period and was privatised between 1992 and 1999. The largest Polish bank, PKO, is still somewhat of a state-owned bank, the ultimate owner of it being the Polish Treasury. In all the three countries, the five largest banks account for about 60% of the total banking sector in terms of assets. All the ranked banks of the Czech Republic are foreign owned. Although in Poland and Hungary the first largest banks are domestic, the rest of the ranked foreign banks represent 42.9% and 34.2% respectively of the total assets of banking markets in these countries. Thus, Table 8 indicates that the banking sectors in the three countries have the characteristics of extensive foreign ownership.

A similar trend of excessive foreign ownership applies for Estonia, Lithuania and Slovakia. In Estonia, the four largest banks are foreign owned (accounting for 97.8% of banking market) while in Slovakia all the banks have controlling foreign ownership. Slovenia, on the contrary, demonstrates strong domestic holdings in banking, related to the state ownership in banking. The largest banks in Latvia and Malta have both domestic and foreign ownership among the largest banks. In Latvia the largest bank is Parekss Banka[6] which is owned by two Latvian residents. For Cyprus, the banks' data on their ownership structure and market shares was available only to a limited extent. Limited data availability did not allow provision for a more adequate picture on the largest banks in

---

[6] Table 8 does not provide information on ownership because at the end of 2001 the ownership structure was not clear and the exact controlling ownership could not be identified (50% of the shares was held by two private individuals and the remaining 50% held via unknown non-resident holding). Today, the two private shareholders own controlling interest in the bank.

Table 8. Largest Banks and Banking Groups in New Member States as of 31 December 2001

		Largest Banks and Banking Groups				EU Bank-Insurance Group Linkage	
Country		Name	Total Assets (EUR Mio)	Controlling Ownership	Market Share (%)	Name	Country
CZ	1	Ceskoslovenska Obchodni Banka–CSOB	18 709	foreign	21.9	Almanij	BE
CZ	2	Ceska Sporitelna A.S.	15 384	foreign	18	Erste Bank	AT
CZ	3	Komercni Banka	13 501	foreign	15.8	Societe Generale	FR
CZ	4	HVB Bank Czech Republic AS	4 944	foreign	5.8	Munich Re Group	DE
CZ	5	GE Capital Bank A.S.	2 456	foreign	2.9	x	x
CY	1	Bank of Cyprus Group	13 393	NA	40	x	x
CY	2	Cyprus Popular Bank Limited–Laiki Bank	8 426	NA	30	x	x
CY	3	Credit Suisse First Boston (Cyprus) Ltd	5 018	foreign	NA	x	x
CY	4	Hellenic Bank Ltd.	3 941	NA	NA	x	x
CY	5	Alpha Bank Limited	1 907	foreign	8	Alpha Bank AE	GR
EE	1	HansaBank–Hansapank	4 602	foreign	58	Foereningssparbanken–Swedbank	SE
EE	2	Eesti Uhispank–Union Bank of Estonia	1 148	foreign	26	Skandinaviska Enskilda Banken AB	SE
EE	3	Sampo Bank	347	foreign	7.5	Sampo Plc.	FI
EE	4	Nordea Bank Estonia Branch	280	foreign	6.3	Nordea AB	SE
EE	5	Eesti Krediidipank–Estonian Credit Bank	58	domestic	1.5	x	x
HU	1	N. Savings and Comm. Bank–OTP Bank	9 311	domestic	24.1	x	x
HU	2	K&H Bank-Kereskedelmi es Hitelbank	4 666	foreign	12.1	Almanij	BE
HU	3	Hungarian Foreign Trade Bank–MKB	3 706	foreign	9.6	x	x
HU	4	CIB Bank–Central-European Intern.Bank	2 636	foreign	6.8	Banca Intesa Spa	IT
HU	5	HVB Bank Hungary RT	2 195	foreign	5.7	Munich Re Group	DE
LT	1	Vilniaus Bankas	1 759	foreign	39.5	Skandinaviska Enskilda Banken AB	SE
LT	2	AB Bankas Hansa–LTB	892	foreign	30.5	Foereningssparbanken–Swedbank	SE
LT	3	Agricultural Bank of Lith.–Lietuvos Z.U.Bankas	502	foreign	10	x	x

		Bank	Assets	Ownership	%	Parent company		Country
LT	4	Bankas Snoras	252	NA	5.8		x	x
LT	5	AB Ukio Bankas	220	foreign	4		x	x
LV	1	Parekss Banka–Parex Bank	1 198	NA	20		x	x
LV	2	Latvijas Unibanka–Unibank of Latvia	1 052	foreign	18	Skandinaviska Enskilda Banken AB		SE
LV	3	Hansabanka	990	foreign	17	Foereningssparbanken–Swedbank		SE
LV	4	Rietumu Bank Group–Rietumu Banka	558	foreign	9		x	x
LV	5	Latvian Savings Bank–Latvijas KrajBanka	278	domestic	4.1		x	x
MT	1	Bank of Valletta plc	4 329	domestic	46		x	x
MT	2	HSBC Bank Malta Plc	3 655	foreign	39	HSBC Holdings Plc	x	GB
MT	3	Volksbank Malta Ltd	835	foreign	NA		x	x
MT	4	APS Bank Limited	350	domestic	NA		x	x
MT	5	Lombard Bank (Malta) plc	302	foreign	NA		x	x
PL	1	Powsz.Kasa Osz.Bank Polski SA–PKO	22 584	domestic	18.9		x	x
PL.	2	Bank Pekao SA–Bank Polska K.Opicki SA	21 121	foreign	17.7	UniCredito Italiano Spa		IT
PL	3	Bank Przemyslowo–Handlowy PBK SA	13 146	foreign	11	Munich Re Group		DE
PL	4	Bank Handlowy w Warszawie S.A.	9 446	foreign	7.9		x	x
PL	5	ING Bank Slaski S.A.–Capital Group	7 480	foreign	6.3	ING Group		NL
SK	1	Slovak Savings Bank–Slovenska Sporitel'na	4 731	foreign	30	Erste Bank		AT
SK	2	Vseobecna Uverova Banka A.S.	4 097	foreign	20	Banca Intesa Spa		IT
SK	3	Tatra Banka A.S.	2 606	foreign	12	Raiffeisen Zentralbank Oesterr. AG		AT
SK	4	HVB Bank Slovakia A.S.	766	foreign	3.5	Munich Re Group		DE
SK	5	UniBanka A.S.	695	foreign	3	UniCredito Italiano Spa		IT
SL	1	Nova Ljubljanska Banka D.D.	7 788	domestic	28.3		x	x
SL	2	Nova Kreditna Banka Maribor D.D.	2 048	domestic	11.7		x	x
SL	3	SKB Banka DD	1 687	foreign	9.6	Societe Generale		FR
SL	4	Abanka Vipa DD	1 445	domestic	6.5		x	x
SL	5	Banka Koper DD	1 080	domestic	6.3		x	x

Source: annual reports and web pages of listed banks and groups, national banking associations and supervisory authorities, LexisNexis

Cyprus. The shares of the two largest banks, Bank of Cyprus and Laiki Bank, are actively traded on stock exchanges and there is extensive free-float ownership. The third and fifth largest banks in Cyprus have ultimate foreign ownership.

The data suggest that many of the banks in the new member states form parts of some larger EU financial groups. When it comes to the new member states located in Central Europe (e.g., Hungary and the Czech Republic), the EU banking-insurance linkages originate mainly from countries closer to that region (e.g., Germany, Austria and Belgium). In the Czech Republic, the ultimate shareholder of the largest Czech bank, Ceskoslovenska Obchodni Banka (CSOB), is KBC Bank (holding of 81.51%). Thus, the bank forms a part of the Belgian Almanij group. Also Ceska Sporitelna, HVB Bank Czech Republic and Komercni Banka are linked to EU banks and banking groups, accordingly the first two being owned by Bayerische Hypo- und Vereinsbank AG and the latter being ultimately owned by French Société Générale (60% holding). Bayerische Hypo- und Vereinsbank has also banking participation in Hungary and Poland.[7] Belgian KBC Bank and Dutch ABN Amro have holdings in K&H Bank (59% and 40% stake respectively). There are also two Italian holdings among the largest banks in that region: the ultimate stake of Banca IntesaBci in the Hungarian fourth largest bank, CIB-Bank, and the stake of over 50% of UniCredito Italiano Spa in Polish Bank Pekao S.A.

Slovakian banks belong to the EU groups. The Austrian groups, Erste Bank and Raiffeisen Zentralbank Oesterreich AG, hold together a significant 42% stake of the total banking sector assets in Slovakia, followed by the holding of two ranked Italian groups—Banca Intesa Spa and UniCredito Italiano Spa, which account for 23% of banking assets. On the contrary, in Slovenia, only one EU banking-insurance group—French Société Générale—is linked to the largest banking businesses of the country.

The three Baltic States have close linkages with Swedish banking-insurance groups Foereningssparbanken-Swedbank and Skandinaviska Enskilda Banken. In Latvia and Lithuania these linkages are created through direct holdings of two Estonian banks—Hansapank and Eesti Ühispank—that are 100% owned subsidiaries of Swedbank and Skandinaviska Enskilda Banken respectively. Additionally, another Swedish

---

[7] The bank has participation in HVB Bank in Hungary and Bank Przemyslowo-Handlowy PBK SA in Poland (71% stake).

group—Nordea AB—has a linkage with Estonia in the form of a branch office through its Finnish banking subsidiary, Nordea Bank Finland Plc. The third largest bank in Estonia, Sampo Bank, is directly linked to Finnish group Sampo Plc.

Data available on Cyprus allows a defining linkage between the fifth largest bank in Cyprus, Alpha Bank Ltd., and the Greek banking-insurance group Alpha Bank AE. This reflects the location-related connections between Cyprus and Greece. It is interesting to note that the largest Cypriot banks—Bank of Cyprus Group and Laiki Bank—have a relatively strong presence in Greece. Malta's domestic market is dominated by two main banks, HSBC Malta and Bank of Valletta, which together control around 85% of the consumer banking market. Two other privately owned commercial banks—Lombard Bank (Malta) and APS Bank—operate on a smaller scale. The largest banks on Malta have foreign linkages but most of them do not form parts of the EU financial groups. The only important connection with the EU groups is the second ranked bank HSBC Bank Malta Plc. but it accounts for a significant 39% of the total banking market assets.

Additionally, the three largest member states have some more banks that are not indicated in Table 8 but are important in relation to linkages with the EU banking-insurance groups. In the Czech Republic, Austrian groups have presence through two important credit institutions: Raiffeisenbank (with total assets of 1,863 EUR million) is ultimately controlled by Raiffeisen Zentralbank Oesterreich AG, and the tenth largest bank Stavebni Sporitelna (with total assets of EUR 1,072 million) is owned by Erste Bank. The eighth largest bank in the country, Ceskomoravska Zarucni a Rozvojova Banka is ultimately owned by Belgian KBC Bank N.V. and belongs to the Almanij group.

Raiffeisen Zentralbank Oesterreich AG is also represented in Hungary, having the majority stake in the seventh largest bank, Raiffeisen Bank (with total assets of EUR 1,882 million). The sixth largest bank in Hungary, ABN Amro Magyar (with total assets of 1,890 million EUR) is a wholly owned subsidiary of Dutch ABN Amro. As for Poland, Belgian Almanij has a presence in the country, owning the majority stake of the eighth largest bank—Kredyt Bank (with total assets of 6,333 million EUR)—via its Belgian banking business, KBC Bank N.V. Surprisingly, Allied Irish Banks Plc. has a major shareholding (70%) in the sixth largest bank in Poland, relatively significant Bank Zachodni WBK (with total assets of 7,064 million EUR).

Graph 5 presents the market shares of the 5 largest banks in the new member states (excluding Cyprus and Malta for which the data related to market shares was incomplete). Graph 5 also reflects the total assets of the EU-related banks among the five largest banks in each country. The data suggest that the EU-linked consolidation is strongest in Estonia where the total assets of the EU-linked banks account for 97.8% of the total banking market. The figures for market shares of the EU-linked banks are also relatively high in Lithuania (70%), Slovakia (68.5%) and the Czech Republic (61.5%).

The results of the study indicate that the countries are strongly influenced by possible changes in the relevant EU banking-insurance groups and the EU financial sector in general. On the other hand, the changes in the banks and financial sectors in those new member states can be transferred to the linked EU institutions. Thus, the described extensive linkages can be considered in the light of systemic stability issues.

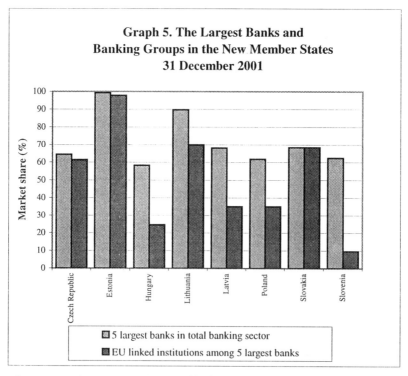

Sources: annual reports and web pages of banks, national banking associations and supervisory authorities, LexisNexis, own calculations

3.2.2. Largest Insurance Undertakings in the New Member States and the European Union Linkages

Table 9 presents the largest insurance undertakings, also indicating ultimate control of either domestic or foreign shareholders and showing the linkages with the EU banking-insurance groups. Previous examination has shown that the financial sectors of the new member states are highly bank dominant. Although the role of insurance activities is relatively modest in the new member states, there is strong growth potential for insurance sectors in the larger states with large markets. Generally, life insurance is less developed compared to non-life insurance and accounts for a relatively modest share of the countries' insurance market in terms of gross written premiums. The exceptional cases are Cyprus and Poland. The former has mostly life-insurers among largest insurance undertakings and the latter shows a significant market share for the second largest insurance firm—life insurer PZU Zycie S.A. The book covers insurance sectors in the new member states without distinguishing between life and non-life insurance because the insurance sectors themselves are small and not considerably important.

The data on the largest new member states suggest that the first largest insurers in Poland and the Czech Republic are controlled by domestic capital, accounting for 54.6% and 38.4% respectively of assets of insurance market in total. Poland and the Czech Republic reflect similar trends of domestic consolidation since the largest insurers in both countries are large domestic groups.[8] Hungary, on the other hand, represents extensive presence of foreign-owned insurance companies among the country's largest insurers. The four largest insurers (with 1,211 million EUR of gross written premiums in total) are foreign-owned and form parts of the EU banking-insurance groups.

In Slovenia the situation in insurance is similar to banking: the largest insurers are only domestic controlled. The Slovak insurance market is dominated by domestic Slovenska Poistovna AS with 46% of the market share while the rest of the insurance undertakings are foreign controlled. When it comes to the three Baltic States, Lithuania shows the strongest market concentration. The Lithuanian subsidiary of Danish Codan AS—Lietuvos Draudimas—accounts for 33% of premiums in the Lithuanian

---

[8] Both Polish PZU companies belong to domestic PZU Group and Czech Ceska Pojistovna AS belongs to a large domestic financial services provider PPF Group.

Table 9. Largest Insurance Undertakings in the New Member States as of 31 December 2001

Country	Largest Insurance Undertakings				EU Bank-Insurance Group Linkage		
	Name	Gross Premiums Written (EUR Mio)	Controlling Ownership	Market Share (%)	Name		Country
CZ 1	Ceska Pojistovna AS	971	domestic	38.4		x	X
CZ 2	Kooperativa Pojistovna AS	425	foreign	16.8		x	X
CZ 3	Allianz Pojistovna AS	228	foreign	9	Allianz AG		DE
CZ 4	IBP Pojistovna AS	174	domestic	6.8		x	x
CZ 5	ING-National Nederlanden	133	foreign	5.2	ING Group		NL
CY 1	Laiki CypriaLife	24	NA	16		x	x
CY 2	Eurolife	22	NA	14.6		x	x
CY 3	Universal Life Insurance	21	NA	14		x	x
CY 4	Laiki Insurance	11	NA	7		x	x
CY 5	Alico AIG Life	9	NA	6		x	x
EE 1	AS Sampo Eesti Varakindlustus*	32	foreign	31	Sampo Plc.		FI
EE 2	ERGO Kindlustuse AS	22	foreign	19	Munich Re Group		DE
EE 3	Seesam RV Kindlustuse AS	15	foreign	13		x	x
EE 4	Hansapanga Kindlustuse AS	11	foreign	9.6	Foereningssparbanken–Swedbank		SE
EE 5	Salva Kindlustus AS	7	domestic	6.1		x	x
HU 1	Allianz Hungaria	488	foreign	28.6	Allianz AG		DE
HU 2	Generali–Providencia Biztosito Rt	291	foreign	17.1	Generali Assicurazioni Spa		IT
HU 3	AB-AEGON Altalanos Biztosito Rt	218	foreign	12.8	Aegon N.V.		NL
HU 4	ING Nationale–Nederlanden	214	foreign	12.6	ING Group		NL
HU 5	OTP–Garancia Biztosito Rt	172	domestic	10.1		x	x

		Company				Group		
LT	1	Lietuvos Draudimas	42	foreign	33		x	X
LT	2	Ergo Lietuva	12	foreign	9.5	Munich Re Group	x	DE
LT	3	Lietuvos Draudimo Gyvybes Draudimas	11	foreign	8.7		x	X
LT	4	Preventa	7	foreign	5.6	Munich Re Group	x	DE
LT	5	If Draudimas	6	foreign	4.8	Sampo Plc.		FI
LV	1	AG Balta	36	foreign	21		x	X
LV	2	ERGO AG	31	foreign	18	Munich Re Group		DE
LV	3	BTA	23	domestic	13.5		x	X
LV	4	Parekss AK	19	NA	11		x	X
LV	5	BALVA	15	foreign	8.8		x	X
MT	1	Middle Sea Insurance Plc	61	NA	NA		x	X
PL	1	Powszechny Zaklad Ubezpieczen SA PZU	2 143	domestic	33.6		x	X
PL	2	PZU Zycie S.A.	1 919	domestic	21		x	X
PL	3	Commercial Union Polska	710	foreign	7.8	Aviva Plc		GB
PL	4	TuiR Warta S.A.	694	domestic	7.6		x	X
PL	5	Amplico-Life S.A.	392	foreign	4.3		x	X
SK	1	Slovenska Poistovna A.S.	467	domestic	46		x	X
SK	2	Kooperativa Pojistovna AS	97	foreign	9.5		x	X
SK	3	Allianz Pojistovna AS	84	foreign	8.3	Allianz AG		DE
SK	4	Prvá americko-slovenská poisťovňa a. s.	83	foreign	8.2		x	X
SK	5	Nationale-Nederlanden Poisťovňa a. s.	59	foreign	5.8	ING Group		NL
SL	1	Triglav Insurance Company	424	domestic	41		x	X
SL	2	Health Insurance Mutual	216	domestic	21		x	X
SL	3	Maribor Insurance Company	134	domestic	13		x	X
SL	4	Adriatic Insurance Company	99	domestic	9.5		x	X
SL	5	Reinsurance Co. Sava Ltd	56	domestic	5.4		x	X

*In 2002, AS Sampo Eesti Varakindlustus was renamed If Eesti Kindlustus AS.

Source: annual reports and web pages of listed insurance undertakings and groups, national insurance associations and supervisory authorities, LexisNexis

market. There is a relatively strong presence of foreign ownership among the insurers in Lithuania and Estonia, and the largest insurers are mostly subsidiaries of some European insurance group (e.g., Codan, Munich Re, Pohjola Group[9]).

The research results for the insurance sector in Cyprus reflect strong linkages between local banking and insurance, and suggest that the financial services sector is greatly dominated by a few players. Thus, the results for the insurance sector significantly coincide with the research results for the banking sector. Four ranked insurance undertakings are part of Cypriot largest banking groups Laiki Bank and the Bank of Cyprus Group. In Malta, the financial institutions operate under conditions of open competition. While developments in the Maltese banking sector in 1999 and onwards can be described by foreign banks having invested in local banks and acquired minority shares, the opposite has occurred in the insurance sector: local Maltese companies have expanded abroad.[10] Since complete figures on the insurance sector in Malta were not available, Table 9 covers only the major insurance company—Middle Sea Insurance Plc. The company is not part of any EU banking-insurance group.

There is a rationale for the suggestion that the EU groups have chosen to participate[11] in insurance undertakings in the new member states but not to have controlling ownership since the insurance sectors have smaller importance and some new member states are influenced by specific conditions (e.g., former strong state-ownership and following privatisation of companies in Poland).

In comparison with the largest banks in the new member states, the data suggest that there are fewer linkages with the EU banking-insurance groups among largest insurance undertakings. However, foreign control among the ranked insurance undertakings is relatively extensive. The reason for such controversy can be found in the form and way of foreign control. The research results indicate that some of the ranked foreign-

---

[9] The subsidiary of Pohjola Group in Estonia is Seesam RV Kindlustuse AS.

[10] S. Smid, S. Noordam, "Financial Services on Malta: Study on the Situation of Enterprises, the Industry and the Service Sectors in Turkey, Cyprus and on Malta." December 2002, p. 6.

[11] Some groups participate through associations. The best examples are Powszechny Zaklad Ubezpieczen SA–PZU which is an associated company of Dutch Eureko B.V. with 21% of stake and TuIR Warta SA which is an associated firm of Belgian Almanij (through KBC Insurance) with 40% of stake.

controlled undertakings form parts of large European insurance groups[12] or outside-EU businesses which are not the banking-insurance groups defined in the research objectives of this book.

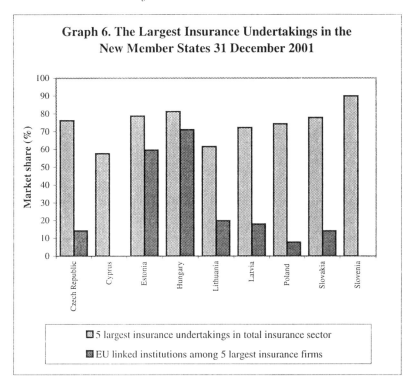

Graph 6. The Largest Insurance Undertakings in the New Member States 31 December 2001

□ 5 largest insurance undertakings in total insurance sector

▨ EU linked institutions among 5 largest insurance firms

Sources: annual reports and web pages of insurance undertakings, national insurance authorities, LexisNexis, own calculations

Graph 6 reflects that the largest insurance firms in the new member states account on average for 75 % of the local insurance markets in terms of gross premiums written. Thus, insurance markets in the new member states are relatively concentrated and divided among larger "players." Compared to the relatively strong EU linkages of the largest banks, the insurance providers of the new member states are significantly less EU-linked. It is interesting to classify the new member states into

[12] For example, Czech Kooperativa Pojistovna is a subsidiary of Austrian Wiener Stadtische Versicherung and Latvian AG Balta is a subsidiary of Danish Codan (belonging to Royal & Sun Alliance group).

three different categories according to the origin of their EU linkage and significance on the local market: insurance markets with the EU-linked dominance, insurance markets with the presence of the EU linkages and insurance markets with no (or very few) EU linkages.

The data suggest that in Hungary and Estonia the gross insurance premiums of the largest insurance undertakings are written mostly by undertakings belonging to some EU linked banking-insurance group.[13] These two countries have clear dominance of EU-linked undertakings in terms of market share. On the other hand, Cyprus and Slovenia as insurance markets with no (or very few) EU linkages have no EU-linked undertakings among the five largest insurance providers which amount for 57.6% and 90% respectively of the total insurance markets. Latvia, Lithuania, Poland and Slovakia show some presence of the EU-linked undertakings, but a larger part of gross premiums is written either by single domestic undertakings, domestic groups or foreign firms outside the definition of the EU banking-insurance groups.

3.2.3. Presence of the European Union Banking-Insurance Groups in the New Member States

Previous examinations indicate that most of the large EU banking-insurance groups have significant business undertakings in the new member states. The banking sectors of the new member states are strongly EU-related and dominated by banks/banking groups that belong to some large EU group. My previous examinations result in the conclusion that in addition to relatively strong connections between the institutions in the EU and the new member states, the related EU entities are generally important "players" in the new member states and have important roles in local markets. This applies particularly to banking which is the most important and dominant part of financial sectors in the new member states. In the following part of the book a brief overview of the presence of EU banking-insurance groups in the new member states is presented. Thereafter the book examines the linkage-creation and developments between the EU and the new member states with strong focus on related M&A activities.

---

[13] The EU-linked gross written premiums amount for 71% in Hungary and 60% in Estonia of the total insurance markets.

Table 10. Banking–Insurance Groups in the New Member States as of 31 December 2001

EU BANKING-INSURANCE GROUP		Presence in the New Member States									
NAME	Country	CZ	CY	EE	HU	LT	LV	MT	PL	SK	SL
1 Deutsche Bank AG*	DE	x			x				x		
2 Allianz AG	DE	x			x				x	x	
3 BNP Paribas	FR	x	x		x				x	x	
4 HSBC Holdings Plc	GB	x	x					x	x		
5 ING Group–Internationale Nederlanden Groep NV	NL	x			x				x	x	
6 ABN Amro Holding NV	NL	x							x		
7 The Royal Bank of Scotland Group Plc	GB										
8 Barclays Plc	GB		x								
9 Crédit Agricole CA	FR				x				x		
10 Société Générale	FR	x									x
11 Fortis	BE								x		
12 AXA	FR	x							x		
13 HBOS Plc	GB										
14 DZ Bank AG-Deutsche Zentral-Gen.bank	DE				x				x		
15 Santander Central Hispano	ES	x			x						
16 Dexia	BE									x	
17 Banca Intesa SpA	IT				x				x	x	
18 Lloyds TSB Group Plc	GB										
19 Banco Bilbao Vizcaya Argentaria SA	ES										
20 Abbey National Plc	GB										
21 Aviva Plc	GB	x	x		x	x		x	x		
22 Groupe Caisse d'Epargne	FR										
23 Aegon NV	NL				x						
24 Almanij	BE	x			x				x		x
25 Prudential Plc	GB										
26 Nordea AB	SE	x		x	x	x	x		x	x	x
27 Generali Assicurazioni SpA	IT	x			x			x	x	x	x
28 Credit Mutuel–CIC	FR										
29 Danske Bank A/S	DK								x		
30 UniCredito Italiano SpA	IT	x			x				x	x	x
31 Crédit Lyonnais	FR	x			x				x	x	
32 Groupe Banques Populaires	FR	x			x			x	x	x	x
33 Munich Re Group	DE	x		x	x	x	x		x	x	
34 San Paolo IMI	IT				x						
35 Standard Life Assurance Company	GB										
36 Svenska Handelsbanken	SE								x		

EU BANKING-INSURANCE GROUP		Presence in the New Member States									
NAME	Country	CZ	CY	EE	HU	LT	LV	MT	PL	SK	SL
37 Skandinaviska Enskilda Banken AB	SE			x		x	x		x		
38 Gruppo Monte dei Paschi di Siena	IT										
39 Foereningssparbanken–Swedbank	SE			x		x	x				
40 Banca Nazionale del Lavoro SA–BNL	IT										
41 Caja de Ahorros y Pens. de Barcelona	ES										
42 Allied Irish Banks plc	IE								x		
43 Erste Bank	AT	x			x					x	
44 Caixa Geral de Depositos	PT										
45 Skandia Insurance Company Ltd.	SE		x						x		
46 Groupama	FR				x						
47 Eureko B.V.	NL		x						x		
48 Wuestenrot & Wuertembergisse AG	DE	x			x				x	x	
49 National Bank of Greece SA	GR		x								
50 BAWAG PSK Group	AT									x	X
51 Raiffeisen Zentralbank Oesterreich AG	AT	x			x	x			x	x	X
52 SNS Reaal Groep	NL										
53 Espirito Santo Financial Group S.A.	LU										
54 Irish Life & Permanent Plc	IE										
55 Alpha Bank AE	GR		x								
56 Okobank Group	FI			x							
57 Sampo Plc	FI			x		x	x		x		
58 Banco BPI SA	PT										
59 Commercial Bank of Greece	GR		x								
60 Compagnia Assicuratrice Unipol SpA	IT										

Source: annual reports and web pages of listed banking-insurance groups, LexisNexis

Table 10 explains the presence of the EU banking-insurance groups in the new member states. The presence is determined according to controlling interest[14] of the EU groups in undertakings of the new member states. In addition to direct banking and insurance activities in the new member states, I have also included other financial activities (e.g., leasing and investments) into the overview provided in Table 10. The all-inclusive ap-

[14] The EU banking-insurance groups are defined to have a presence in the new member states, if they are ultimate shareholders (usually over 50% of holding) in relevant entities.

proach is mainly based on my assumption that once the EU groups have established some financial business in the new member states, there is a strong potential for further expansion of their service provision. Thus, it is very likely that the groups involved in some other field of financial business are also to expand into banking and insurance business. Table 10 also covers representative offices of the EU banking-insurance groups. The assumption is that the presence of a representative office is also a clear indicator of further expansion intentions. Thus, Table 10 is tailored to provide both on the spot and forward-looking positions in order to understand the relevant linkages and interest of the EU banking-insurance groups in the new member states.

Table 10 suggests that there are no universal group characteristics that trigger the expansion into many countries. Larger groups (e.g., HSBC Holding) and smaller groups (e.g., Sampo Plc.), insurance-headed groups (e.g., Aviva Plc) and bank-headed groups (e.g., Nordea AB), private commercial groups (e.g., Munich Re) and special-structured groups (e.g., Raiffeisen Zentralbank Oesterreich AG) have linkages with a number of the new member states. However, one can recognise a few country-specific aspects.

Although ranked among largest in terms of assets, UK-based groups have relatively little presence in the new member states while large German groups have expanded their business very extensively. One of the reasons is likely to be that the UK is relatively separate and does not have geographically or traditionally very strong connections with the new member states. The financial markets in the UK are highly developed and offer great opportunities for the institutions. Additionally, it is the case that the UK institutions are very active in most of the world's attractive markets. The benefits of operating highly-capitalized institutions either in the UK, USA or any other promising market (e.g., Asia) certainly determine the focus of business. Thus, there is apparently lesser need for the expansion into the relatively small and unknown new member states. The countries such as Germany, Austria, Belgium and the Netherlands, on the other hand, are located closer to the new member states and have connections with many of them for geographical, traditional and historical reasons.

Spanish and Portuguese groups have almost no presence[15] in the new member states, one of the reasons certainly being those states' very different cultural and linguistic environment. Greece and France represent spe-

---

[15] Banco BPI SA has quite recently acquired a 50 % stake in Polish Bank Millenium. Table 10 does not reflect this transaction.

cific cases: the groups of Greece have presence only in closely situated and culturally similar Cyprus while the presence of French groups depends much on whether they are commercial groups or specific groups with a mutual-undertaking structure.[16] When it comes to Scandinavian groups, Swedish and Finnish groups have linkages with a number of new member states (e.g., Nordea AB, which doesn't have presence only in Cyprus and on Malta) while Danske Bank A/S has its business only in Poland.

It is important to note that Table 10 does not reflect the interests of some groups because they did not have ultimate ownership at the end of 2001. However, taking into consideration future developments and continuous interest of the EU banking-insurance groups in the new member states, it is certainly important to highlight some of those linkages. Austrian BAWAG PSK Group has participating interests in Hungarian and Czech banks but these banks are not treated as operating companies of BAWAG PSK Group and they are not reflected in Table 10. The table reflects BAWAG's interest in Slovakia that was achieved at the end of 2001 by acquiring 100 % in Slovak Istrobanka. Another important group, whose interest is not included in Table 10, is the Italian-originated San Paolo IMI that had a 15% stake in Slovenian Banka Koper at the end of 2001. However, after 2001 the situation changed and San Paolo IMI increased its stake to 61% of Banka Koper in 2003. Additionally, Dutch Eureko has strategic holding in the largest Polish insurer PZU, which Eureko treats as its associate company and has declared its continuous interest in. All these linkages support the conclusion that the new member states are an attractive market for the EU banking-insurance groups.

Graph 7 seeks to explain the country linkages between the EU and the new member states. Graph 7 is based on the previously determined connections and shows which new member states are linked to which EU countries in terms of presence of the EU banking-insurance groups.

Graph 7 clearly indicates the relevance of market size in particular countries: larger new member states have connections with more EU countries than smaller states because larger markets are more attractive and allow the presence of more players. Poland seems to be the most attractive market for the EU banking-insurance groups and has linkages with 11 EU countries. Poland is followed by the Czech Republic and Hungary that are both linked to nine EU countries. The data suggest that German, Dutch, Belgian and French groups have a presence in the new

---

[16] Institutions with a mutual-undertaking structure mainly operate locally.

member states which are located in Central Europe (e.g., Poland, the Czech Republic and Slovakia) while Scandinavian groups have strong preference in geographically and culturally closer Baltic States. Malta and Cyprus, smaller and geographically southern new member states, have respectedly fewer linkages. Additionally, both Malta and Cyprus have links with the UK and France—old member states that have presence in the two countries with few other EU-linkages.

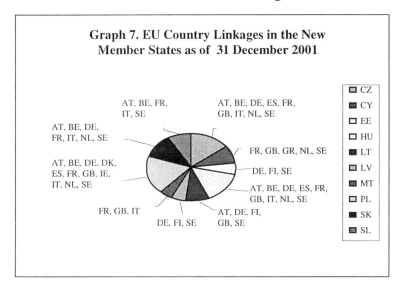

Graph 7. EU Country Linkages in the New Member States as of 31 December 2001

Sources: annual reports and web-pages of EU banking-insurance groups, LexisNexis, own calculations

One can draw a conclusion that besides institution-specific and economic factors (such as economies of scale, level of sophistication and leading market position), a few country-specific aspects such as location, traditions, historical and cultural issues have played certain role in cross-border expansion into the new member states. The new member states have been, currently are and most probably will continue to be an attractive investment area for the EU banking-insurance groups.

3.3. M&A Activities of the European Union Banking-Insurance Groups in the New Member States

3.3.1. Banking-Insurance Sector M&A Experience

In the past few years, the impact of M&As in the banking industry in Central and Eastern Europe has been that most domestic banks have already become or are likely to become subsidiaries of large foreign banks. In the wake of massive privatization programs, foreign banks have rapidly taken control over the domestic banking industry in this region. M&A deals within foreign banks might lead to increased concentration of the banking industry in countries where they are operating through their subsidiaries. For example, the announced but cancelled merger of the top two Swedish banks, Swedbank and SEB was expected to lead to a further consolidation of the banking industry in the Baltic region. Together, these two banks control more than 70 % of the Lithuanian banking market. Similarly the combined market share is high in Estonia where the groups control as much as around 85 % of the total bank assets.[17] Strongly related to the developments in banking, the most common form of the EU banking-insurance groups' business expansion into the new member states has been M&A activities. In the following, I will examine intersector M&A activities across the borders of the new member states and seek to determine the major M&A criteria of those developments.

Table 11 covers M&A transactions initiated by the EU banking-insurance groups and aimed at acquiring banks/insurance undertakings in the new member states. I have defined the major M&A deals that have allowed the EU banking-insurance groups to achieve control or relatively strong participating interests in relevant businesses in the new member states. The deals presented in Table 11 mostly reflect acquisitions of local businesses by the EU banking-insurance groups and have resulted in substantial control over target banks/insurance firms of the new member states. I have taken into consideration only directly EU-initiated acquisitions, i.e. those acquisitions that are completed by any EU-located banking-insurance group. I have not looked at the deals initiated by the groups' subsidiaries located in some of the new member states. Transaction data is provided for the years 1990–2002 and the transactions are

---

[17] K. Singh, "Global Corporate Power: Emerging Trends and Issues." *Asia–Pacific Journal*, No. 4, June 2001.

Table 11. M&A Activities of EU Banking-Insurance Groups in New Member States, 1990–2002

ACQUIRER		TARGET		Transaction Year(s)
EU Banking-Insurance Group	Country	Bank/Insurance Firm in the New Member State	Country	
1 Allianz AG	DE	Hungaria Biztosito Rt	HU	1990
2 Generali Assicurazioni Spa	IT	AB-Generali Budapest Biztosito	HU	1991
3 Aegon NV	NL	Allami Biztosito	HU	1992
4 ING Group	NL	Bank Slaski w Katowicach	PL	1994, 1996, 2001
5 Bayerische Hypo-und Vereinsbank*	DE	MegaBank Financial	PL	1995
6 Aegon NV	NL	AB Aegon	HU	1995
7 ABN Amro Holding NV	NL	Interbank	PL	1995
8 ABN Amro Holding NV	NL	Magyar Hitel Bank	HU	1996
9 Allied Irish Banks Plc	IE	Wielkopolski Bank Kredytowy	PL	1996–1997
10 Credit Lyonnais	FR	International Bank of Poland	PL	1997
11 ABN Amro Holding NV	NL	MeesPierson EurAmeroca	HU	1997
12 Erste Bank	AT	Mezobank Rt	HU	1997
13 Credit Lyonnais	FR	Credit Lyonnais Bank Polska	PL	1998
14 BAWAG PSK Group	AT	Magyar Kulkereskedelmi Bank	HU	1998
15 Alpha Bank AE	GR	Lombard NatWest Bank	CY	1998
16 Allianz AG	DE	Allianz BGZ Polska SA	PL	1998
17 Bayerische Hypo- und Vereinsbank*	DE	Bank Przemyslovo-Handlowy SA	PL	1998–1999
18 Skandinaviska Enskilda Banken	SE	Vilniaus Bank	LT	1998, 2000
19 Skandinaviska Enskilda Banken	SE	Eesti Ühispank	EE	1998, 2000
20 Skandinaviska Enskilda Banken	SE	Latvijas Unibanka	LV	1998, 2000
21 Foereningssparbanken-Swedbank	SE	Hansapank	EE	1998–2002

22 Almanij	BE	Ceskoslovenska Obchodni Banka	CZ	1999
23 HSBC Holdings	GB	Mid-Med Bank Plc	MT	1999
24 Fortis	BE	Pierwszy Polko-Amerykanski Bank	PL	1999
25 DZ Bank AG	DE	Bank Ameykanski w Polsce SA	PL	1999
26 Credit Agricole	FR	Credigen Penzugyi Szolgaltato	HU	1999
27 Almanij	BE	Agropolisa SA	PL	1999
28 Almanij	BE	Chmelarska Pojistovna	CZ	1999
29 Wuestenrot & Wuertembergisse AG	DE	Lakaskassza	HU	2000
30 UniCredito Italiano Spa	IT	Polnobanka AS	SK	2000
31 Skandinaviska Enskilda Banken	SE	Bank Ochrony Srodowiska	PL	2000
32 Sampo Plc	FI	Powzechne Towarzystwo	PL	2000
33 Sampo Plc	FI	Norwich Union Towarzystwo	PL	2000
34 Sampo Plc	FI	Development Bank	LT	2000
35 Sampo Plc	FI	Optiva Bank AS	EE	2000
36 Raiffeisen Zentralbank Oesterr. AG	AT	Polonia SA	PL	2000
37 Nordea AB	SE	Bank Kommunalny w Gdyni SA	PL	2000
38 Nordea AB	SE	Societe Generale-Lativan	LV	2000
39 Nordea AB	SE	Societe Generale-Lithuanian	LT	2000
40 Dexia	BE	Prva Kommunalna Banka	SK	2000
41 Deutsche Bank AG	DE	Bank Wspolpracy Regionalnej S.	PL	2000
42 Danske Bank A/S	DK	Polsko-Kanadyjski Bank Sw	PL	2000
43 Almanij	BE	Hungarian Coml. And Credit Bank	HU	2000
44 Erste Bank	AT	Ceska Sporitelna	CZ	2000–2002
45 Societe Generale	FR	Komercni Banka AS	CZ	2001
46 Societe Generale	FR	SKB Banka dd	SL	2001
47 Munich Re	DE	Preventa (Ergo Hestia)	LT	2001

48	Erste Bank	AT	Slovenska Sporitelna	SK	2001
49	Banca Intesa Spa	IT	Vseobecna Uverova Banka	SK	2001
50	Almanij	BE	K&H Eletbiztosito	HU	2001
51	Allianz AG	DE	Slovenska Poistovna	SK	2001
52	Allianz AG	DE	Bank Powierniczo-Gwarancyjny	PL	2001
53	Almanij	BE	Kredyt Bank PBI SA	PL	2001–2002
54	San Paolo IMI	IT	Banka Koper	SL	2002
55	Raiffeisen Zentralbank Oesterr. AG	AT	Krekova Banka	SL	2002
56	Raiffeisen Zentralbank Oesterr. AG	AT	Funeuropa Biztosito	HU	2002
57	Nordea AB	SE	Petrobank	PL	2002
58	Almanij	BE	Nova Ljubljanska Banka	SL	2002

*Bayerische Hypo- und Vereinsbank, which completed the acquisitions, is related to Munich Re
Source: LexisNexis, annual reports and web pages of listed institutions, own modifications in grouping the deals

listed according to their effective date. In some cases (e.g., ING Group's acquisition in Poland; Skandinaviska Enskilda Banken's acquisitions in Lithuania, Latvia and Estonia) Table 11 shows that the acquisitions took place in different phases[18] and during longer periods of time.

The data in Table 11 is in correlation with the data provided previously in Table 10. Most of the EU groups that are covered by Table 10 can be also found in an acquirer's role in Table 11. The most important acquirers are German, Dutch, Swedish, Austrian and Belgian groups. Among the targets there are the largest banks of the new member states (e.g., Ceska Sporitelna, SKB Banka and Hansapank). This clearly explains the trend of extensive foreign ownership among the banks in the new member states. Most of the target companies are traditionally banks and banking institutions. Insurance acquisitions are less frequent. The country with the most of insurance targets is Hungary that has also the highest ratio of the EU-linked ownership in the insurance sector. The acquisitions of insurance companies occurred mainly in the beginning years of the period (e.g., the acquisitions of AB Generali Budapest Biztosító in 1991 and Hungária Biztosító in 1990) and became active again—together with the extensive overall M&A activities—during 1999 to 2002.[19]

When looking at the transaction years, the pattern is similar to M&A trends within the EU: over 50 % of the transactions fall in the period from 2000 to 2002. This is likely to reflect that the years 2000 and 2001 were the most active years of M&A activities in the world. Among the new member states, the most transactions were completed with Polish and Hungarian banks/insurance undertakings while Cypriot and Maltese banks/insurance firms were engaged in only one transaction per country.

Table 11 suggests that M&A activities related to banking and insurance business in the new member states can be classified in three sets of periods, depending on the transaction year and acquirer's nation. The first period comprises of the beginning of the period: from 1990 to 1995. Dutch groups have been the major acquirers. In particular from 1992 to 1995, their acquisitions of Polish and Hungarian banks and insurance firms have contributed to the largest deals.

---

[18] Acquisitions took place through many smaller deals, each related to the acquisition of certain portions of shares.

[19] The examples are the acquisitions of Chmelarska Pojistovna in 1999, Norwich Union Towarzyztwo in 2000 and Slovenska Poistovna in 2001.

In the middle of the observed period, from 1997 to 1999, Belgian, German and Swedish groups were among the major acquirers. Additionally, the activities of Swedish groups in 1998 have specific characteristics, reflecting the start of longer-perspective stake acquisitions[20] in Baltic banks. The strong majority of M&A's falls under the end of the examined period. The end of the period is relatively diversified, with both the acquirers and targets belonging to a large number of nations and the acquisitions aimed at both credit institutions and insurance undertakings.

One can conclude that M&A activities in the new member states have generally followed two patterns. On one hand the advantageous market conditions and favourable legislative/administrative situations in the new member states (i.e. liberalisation in early 1990s and privatisation of financial industry) have increased the interest of the EU groups in the new member states and the attractiveness of financial institutions. On the other hand, general M&A trends in Europe and in the world have also influenced M&A activities in the new member states (e.g., the increased bank and insurance M&A's in the new member states coincide with the trend of extensive worldwide M&A's in 2000 and 2001).

3.3.2. M&A Criteria: Case Studies

Enterprise strategy is generally developed at the board level and asks the questions: "Why are we in this business anyway?" and "Is there anything out there that can better utilise our cash flows?" Thus, a strategy might develop at the enterprise level to expand the enterprise by making a major horizontal acquisition. Alternatively, the option might be to temporarily contract the enterprise by selling off major lines and later reallocating cash flows into entirely new and higher-yielding lines.[21]

We have previously seen that the linkage creation between the EU banking-insurance groups and the new member states has taken place largely in the form of M&As. In the first chapter the book discussed the major reasons why M&As occur. In the following I seek to provide a rationale and reasoning for some major acquisitions of ultimate interest by the EU groups in institutions of the new member states. I have chosen to examine the M&A business of four EU banking-insurance groups, look-

---

[20] The stake acquisitions resulted in the acquisitions of ultimate ownership by 2000.

[21] S. Foster Reed, A. Reed Lajoux, *The Art of M&A: A Merger/Acquisition/Buyout Guide.* McGraw-Hill Companies, New York, 1998, p. 15.

ing at their most important transactions in the new member states. The book will provide short case studies of the four successful M&A strategies: Erste Bank, ING Group, Skandinaviska Enskilda Banken and Allianz AG, addressing their acquisitions in order to discuss the main ideas behind the acquisitions.

CASE I: ERSTE BANK IN THE CZECH REPUBLIC AND SLOVAKIA

Difference in Business Sector Orientation: Building a Retail Network

The difference between the financial sectors of the acquirer nation and target nation has proved to be a driving factor of M&A's. When the acquirer is focused on a certain type of business and the target nation's relevant sector has very weak orientation in that business, the acquirer might want to acquire business undertakings of the relevant sector in order to build up the sector and become a market-leader. The best examples of such M&A strategy are Erste Bank's acquisitions of Ceská Sporitelna in August 2000 (52%) and in August 2002, and Slovenská Sporitelna in January 2001.[22] Erste Bank is a savings bank in Austria. The Austrian banking sector includes banking associations as well as savings banks. Erste Bank is focused on saving and this is the common history for Ceská Sporitelna, Erste Bank and that of Slovenská Sporitelna. Erste Bank's main strategy and goal in the M&A's was to build up a big retail-group, which was something that had not previously existed in Central and Eastern Europe. Erste Bank aimed at becoming a leading retail banking group in Central and Eastern Europe, with a strategic target market being retail businesses and the small and medium-sized enterprises. Based on a long-term experience within retail banking, the inclusion of both Slovenská Sporitelna and Ceská Sporitelna as the main institutions of their kind in Central and Eastern Europe, proved successful for the Erste Bank.

Table 12. Erste Bank Results in Central Europe

	1999	2000	2001	2002
Turnover (EUR Mio)	NA	202,1	569,7	774,9
Profit before tax (EUR Mio)	21,6	30,8	169,4	377,7

Source: LexisNexis

[22] Thomson Financial, *Thomson Extel Cards Database*, 27 June 2003.

The acquisitions of the two large banks in the new member states have led Erste Bank to create an impressive retail network and significantly increase its turnover and profits in Central European new member states. Although the activities of Erste Bank in Central Europe include the activities in the Czech Republic, Hungary, Slovakia, Slovenia and Croatia, these acquisitions in the Czech Republic and Slovakia (respectively initiated in August 2000 and January 2001) are the ones that contribute to the significant improvement of results of Erste Bank in the region.

CASE II: ING GROUP IN POLAND
Strong Country Focus: Creation of a New Home Market
In Europe ING has declared that, among others, its strategic objectives are to build on the strong positions in Poland as an integrated financial services provider.[23] I define a strong country focus as a factor that reflects the group's interest in particular region and triggers M&A activities of the group in that region. A good example of a strong country focus is the Dutch ING Group and its acquisitions in Poland. Table 11 shows ING Group's three-phase acquisition of Bank Slaski w Katowicach. Using Bank Slaski as an acquirer, ING Group has additionally created a presence in other banks in Poland. Those other acquisitions are not considered direct acquisitions by the EU banking-insurance groups and are not reflected in Table 11. However, some of those acquisitions are to illustrate and explain the rationale for a strong country focus of the ING Group. In the context of a strong country focus one can recognise that the ING Group has created a strong presence in Poland and exercised three major group strategies in the country: a significant growth of market share, global brand building and an improvement of competitive edge. Those strategies support focus on Poland and explain that under a strong country focus all important group strategies and developments are to be transferred to target companies. M&A activities with such orientation aim at the creation of another home market.

a) Significant growth of market share

ING Group's strategy in Poland assumed a significant growth of the market share by offering numerous financial services through a variety of distribution channels. The strategic idea was wealth accumulation supported by the efficient mix of channels that were appropriate for client segments and products. The strategy focused on cost reduction. Addition-

---

[23] ING Bank Slaski SA. *Annual Report 2001*. Available: http//www.ing.pl

ally, ING aimed at becoming a market leader in pensions, life and wholesale banking by leveraging its market value.[24] ING completed a subsequent integration of all banking activities into ING Bank Slaski in 2001. In March 2001, the ING Group increased its shareholding in Bank Slaski to 82.8% for an amount of 187 million EUR.[25] All life, employee benefits and pension activities were also integrated. Good preparation and an effective consolidation process allowed the ING Group to achieve the expected effects of synergy and scale. Major improvement of the ING Group's position in the Polish market was the result of ING Bank Slaski organic growth combined with a consolidation processes which I examine as follows.

b) Improvement of competitive edge

In line with the situation in the banking market, ING Bank Slaski actively participated in consolidation. It improved its competitive edge via merging with the ING Bank N.V. Warsaw Branch in September 2001 and the acquisition of Wielkopolski Bank Rolniczy. ING Bank Slaski enhanced its positions especially regarding the market share, capital strength increase and diversification of the operations. The complementary character of merging institutions—the universal nature of ING Bank Slaski and specialisation of the ING Bank N.V., Warsaw Branch in corporate markets—generated substantial benefits for ING Bank Slaski through:

(i)   the growth of capital strength, allowing for implementation of larger projects,

(ii) better market position of the consolidated bank (especially on the corporate banking market) being a premise for more efficient competition on the market as a whole,

(iii) the growth of customer base and the new possibilities of cross-selling,

(iv) the exchange of experience and know-how on different aspects of financial services,

(v)   better diversification of business and better risk control,

(vi) the reduced costs of the head office, information technology systems and back-office,

(vii) better efficiency of marketing efforts and resources.[26]

---

[24] Among other channels, the leveraging of market value of ING Group was done via distribution alliances.

[25] ING Bank Slaski SA. *Annual Report 2001.* Available: http//www.ing.pl

[26] ING Bank Slaski SA. *Annual Report 2001.* Available: http//www.ing.pl

The total consolidated balance sheet of ING Bank Slaski grew by 36% during the year. The main reason for the increase in 2001 was the contribution of the ING Bank N.V. Branch in Warsaw, made on 1 October 2001.[27] From 1 January 2002 to 31 December 2002 the gross consolidated profit before tax increased by 32.5% in comparison to the previous year.[28] The main trigger was the increase of banking operations, caused by the merging of activities with the ING Bank Warsaw Branch at levelled off expenses and provision charges.

c) Global brand building

In the environment of consolidation and ongoing changes in consumer requirements, technology, distribution and legislation, clients look for stability, reliability and familiarity. A strong, universal brand offers a promise to clients in terms of quality, value for money, corporate style and culture. In 2001, Bank Slaski commenced the re-branding process and started operations under the new name of ING Bank Slaski. The re-branding constitutes a part of the long-term strategy of ING Group, whose target is to render integrated financial services and establish the group's image as an innovative, customer-oriented, and dynamic international organisation. Using the global brand of ING is particularly appropriate for a new situation in the banking market which is characterised by an increased significance of a brand as a decisive factor for choosing a bank.

CASE III: SKANDINAVISKA ENSKILDA BANKEN IN ESTONIA, LATVIA AND LITHUANIA
Expansion with "E-centric" Vision

The creation of new home markets and expansion expectations are economically sound rationale that triggers many M&A activities. At the end of 1998, Skandinaviska Enskilda Banken (SEB) entered into a cooperation agreement with three leading Baltic banks—Eesti Ühispank in Estonia, Latvijas Unibanka in Latvia and Vilniaus Bankas in Lithuania. By the end of 1998, SEB also became a part owner of these three banks by acquiring between 32 and 36 per cent of the shares.[29] The purpose was to provide and develop products for both private individuals and compa-

---

[27] ING Bank Slaski SA. *Annual Report 2001.* Available: http//www.ing.pl

[28] ING Bank Slaski SA. *Annual Report 2002.* Available: http//www.ing.pl

[29] Skandinaviska Enskilda Banken. *Annual Report 1998.* Available: http://taz.vv.sebank.se

nies in the Baltic market. Thus, the bank aimed at expansion into the Baltic States.

Table 11 reflects that the acquisition of the Baltic banks was carried on in different phases, resulting in ultimate ownership by 2000. 2001 was the first year during which SEB fully owned the three Baltic banks. SEB had established a solid basis and a strong market share in Baltic countries. SEB's business focused on developing the bank competence, products and efficiency. Co-operation between each respective local bank and the rest of SEB was successful. This led to growing business and increased customer satisfaction. On one hand, SEB's step-by-step acquisitions of the Baltic banks aimed at the expansion, using the obvious growth potential in those countries. There was a great need for universal banking services in the Baltic market, although regional growth had also increased demand for advisory competence and savings products. SEB's current positions allow the expansion to be considered successful. All three banks carry on private advisory activities, selling SEB mutual funds and insurance products. Due to enhanced domestic economy,[30] there has been an increasing need for housing loans and the banks are offering mortgage loans to their private customers. The number of small companies is rapidly growing. Business creation, improved economic situation and advantageous financial conditions have led to increased demand for other types of loans and leasing products.

It is worth noting that besides expansion projection, SEB's M&A strategy across banks in the Baltic States (especially in the last phases of acquisitions) had an additional focus. SEB was a strong performer in internet-based banking services and part of its M&A strategy was the establishment of "e-centric" vision in fast-growing countries. SEB's vision was that the institutions in the Baltic countries are innovative and eager to adopt advanced information technology solutions. The e-based strategy was supported by the argument that introduction and extensive use of internet-based products would have strong effects on cost reduction. SEB's own "e-centric" approach was impressive: at the end of 2001 about 225.000 customers used the Internet for their banking transactions and this reflected an increase of 128 % since the end of 2000. SEB's e-strategy in the Baltic States was successful since all three of SEB's Baltic

---

[30] In addition to an enhanced economic state, there are other factors that trigger growth in housing loans. Currently, the most important motivator seems to be extremely low interest rates.

banks established and exercised aggressive e-banking strategies. Together they had approximately 110,000 Internet customers by the end of the year 2000. Cost reduction proved to be a relevant issue as the number of offices has decreased but the number of transactions has increased.[31] Baltic countries have become extremely innovative and advanced in information technology know-how and developments. Among the pioneers in the market, Eesti Ühispank launched an integrated e-banking and net brokerage service. In October 2001, SEB's Baltic participations received appraisal for innovativeness: Unibanka in Latvia and Vilniaus Bankas in Lithuania were named the best banks in their respective countries for the second year in a row. The assessment was made on the combined basis of profitability, Internet bank, web pages, credit policy and service.

CASE IV: ALLIANZ AG IN HUNGARY
Liberalisation of Emerging Economies
By the beginning of the 1990's, former Soviet bloc countries had achieved or were about to achieve political independence and formation of democratic states. In addition to democratic freedom, these countries also aimed at economic freedom and started to open up their markets in order to switch from a plan-based economy to a market economy. Emerging markets are attractive to investors because of various business opportunities and unused market niches. On the other hand, emerging markets are relatively unstable and investments are thus riskier. Investors in such markets must consider whether investment opportunities outbalance the risk level.

Allianz has a strong international presence and long history in Western Europe. It was one of the first largest financial services providers which invested in Hungary at the beginning of the 1990's. Moreover, the data in Table 11 suggest that Allianz was one of the first acquirers of banking-insurance providers in the new member states. Although it entails higher risks the M&A strategy of Allianz seems economically simple: expanding across emerging markets and benefiting from the liberalisation of the country's economy. Since the political liberalisation, Allianz has actively participated in all insurance segments of the new markets in Central and Eastern Europe.

---

[31] Skandinaviska Enskilda Banken. *Annual Report 1998.* Available: http://taz.vv.sebank.se

Allianz entered the Hungarian market in 1990. During the start of the liberalisation of the country's insurance market it purchased a major share in Hungária Biztosító RT. The strategy of Allianz was to invest in Hungary through the acquisition of ownership in a related services provider—an insurer. Thus, Allianz bought a stake in a local Hungarian insurance company. It is likely that Allianz chose Hungary because of its relative attractiveness for foreign investment compared to other post-soviet countries in the same region. Hungary attracted over $23.6 billion in foreign direct investment (FDI) from 1990–2001, 1995 was a banner year for Hungary with close to $4.5 billion in investment.

Table 13. FDI Inflows in Central and Eastern Europe (USD Mio)

COUNTRY	1990	1991	1992	1993	1994	1995	1996	1997	1998	1999	2000	2001
Czech Republic	72	523	1 003	654	869	2 562	1 428	1 300	3 718	6 324	4 986	4 916
Hungary	311	1 459	1 471	2 339	1 146	4 453	2 275	2 173	2 036	1 944	1 643	2 414
Poland	88	359	678	1 715	1 875	3 659	4 498	4 908	6 365	7 270	9 342	8 830
Slovakia	93	81	100	168	245	195	251	220	684	390	2 075	1 475

Source: Unctad Handbook of Statistics

As we have discussed, emerging markets are riskier but provide for many opportunities. At the time Allianz was the major Western investor in Hungary and served as a leading example for other investors. Additionally, one can assume that Allianz played an important role in the Hungarian economy and had a strong advantage in becoming a large player in the Hungarian insurance market. The ranking of Hungarian largest insurance companies shows that the strategy of Allianz was successful. Allianz Hungaria is the leading insurance company in Hungary, with market share of about 30%. The new member states in Central and Eastern Europe seem to have been one of the key areas of expansion for Allianz AG. It has become the leading foreign insurer and seeks to continue growing its market share in insurance, long-term savings and pension provision.

3.4. Opportunities and Threats of Financial Conglomeration

From the banking industry perspective, the recent results of conglomeration within the EU have shown relatively unexpected results for many large banking groups that have increased their range of financial services and presence in foreign markets. The trend to diversification in the field of large banks will be continuous but diversification has not generated the desired benefits recently because several lines of business have deteriorated at the same time. An increasing importance of retail banking is expected in the markets of the new member states. Due to disintermediation, the share of retail business by banks in the EU is regressive.[32] However, this is to be seen in the light of strongly underperforming financial markets in recent years, when retail business (in particular mortgage lending) of many banks significantly contributed to the support of their overall results.

The overall profitability of European insurance firms, and thus their ability to buffer against risks, started to deteriorate quite markedly in 2001. The negative impact of the stock market fall on insurers—in particular life insurers—is due to their significant equity portfolios, which generally have to be marked to market. As discussed in previous chapters, bancassurance conglomerates have continued to develop in the EU, together with minority shareholdings. Conglomerates carry the potential risk of internal contagion, as problems in the insurance arm might impinge on the capital resources of the bank. Banks may also have capital from the insurance subsidiaries. The relevance of these "conglomerate links" may depend on the organisational structure. In particular, the risks for banks are in most cases mitigated, as the bank and insurance parts are often sister companies under the same holding company, or firewalls are in place preventing the insurance company from influencing banks' capital.[33]

Financial conglomeration has both its positive impacts and drawbacks. Given the diversity of institutions and structural factors that make up the European financial landscape, it would be inappropriate to assume that the potential for benefits that may exist on average will necessarily mean that these benefits will be there for every transaction. Based on the previously examined expansion of the EU institutions across the new member states, I will now discuss the threats that financial conglomeration might create and opportunities that financial conglomeration might offer to institutions and countries involved in conglomeration. The discussion on the opportunities and threats will be combined with addressing the examples of linkage creation between the institutions of the EU and new member states.

[32] C. Eppendorfer, R. Beckmann, M. Neimke, "Market Access Strategies in the EU Banking Sector: Obstacles and Benefits Towards an Integrated European Retail Market." January 2002, pp. 3–5, 10–11.

[33] European Central Bank. *EU Banking Sector Stability.* February 2003, pp. 13, 16–17.

3.4.1. From the Perspective of Institutions

In the first chapter of this book I developed a general discussion on the reasons and mechanics of why and how financial conglomeration takes places. The following pages address the opportunities and threats of financial conglomeration, with focus on the EU conglomeration across the new member states. The two discussions are in line with each other. I have chosen to initiate the two discussions since the objectives of the discussions do not coincide with each other. While the discussion of the first chapter aims at introducing the main principles in general, the following pages seek to provide information and draw conclusions using the former analysis of the EU conglomeration.

From the perspective of institutions one can recognise the following opportunities and threats of conglomeration:

a) Strategic investment

The previous discussions support the statement that M&A activity leading to the conglomeration is usually of the strategic kind. The initiating institution has the purpose of combining a new enterprise or continuing the operations of an existing enterprise. In both cases, the initiator has a longer-term perspective and it looks at further developments and business expansion rather than only cash flows in the close future. From the institution's perspective, such a strategy is beneficial as it enables the combination of new resources (both financial and intellectual) in order to exploit the synergies and to do business in a better and more efficient way. The initiator does not seek to gain fast cash flows and then to get rid of the business but it seeks to expand the group and add value to the organisation in the long run. The previous analyses allow the recognition that the creation of linkages between the EU banking-insurance groups and the new member states has aimed at achieving strategic investment positions in the institutions in the new member states. The EU banking-insurance groups have been seeking to expand and become players in the financial sectors of the new member states (e.g., Almanij in Hungary and the Czech Republic).

b) Diversification

The major advantage of conglomeration relates to income and risk diversification attained from a broader product range and geographic distribution. This is true especially for bancassurance with an ownership element. The flexibility of diversification, when used with necessary caution and diligent management, can contribute to stability of risk diversification and will benefit the different financial sectors included in conglomerates.[34]

It is widely recognised that a larger coverage of geographic areas, industries, types and structures of activities contributes to a reduction in the risk of insolvency. Conglomeration that increases diversification reduces vulnerability to external shocks and thus improves the safety of institutions, whereas an increase in the size of institution *per se* tends to be associated with a greater appetite for risk and a greater probability of insolvency is assumed. Thus, the answer of whether a larger geographical coverage has positive or negative implications is dependent on the initial profiles of the merging institutions, the scale of their operations and the complements in their geographic focus.[35] Indeed, some EU banking-insurance groups have seen advantage in extensively taking their activities into most new member states (e.g., Nordea AB and Munich Re Group), while others have focused only on a particular region which they are familiar with (e.g., the presence of Greek banking-insurance groups in Cyprus).

c) Cost and revenue benefits

I have discussed that conglomeration allows financial groups to achieve cost benefits through cross-selling. Financial groups have the opportunity of efficient use of existing distribution channels and the bringing together of skills from different sectors. Financial conglomeration across the borders of the new member states is a part of international product diversification of the EU financial groups and can lead to revenue enhancement.[36] A good example is the Austrian Erste Bank that has improved its financial state significantly through the expansion of its business into the new member states.

From the future perspective, when the new member states introduce the euro, the institutions face the potential cost benefits created by a single currency. Firms with a substantial presence across several countries within the single currency area might have a cost incentive to consolidate their banking relationship and probably centralise part or all of their treasury and other financial operations.

---

[34] European Central Bank. *Mergers and Acquisitions Involving the EU Banking Industry—Facts and Implications.* December 2000, pp. 30–31.

[35] Group of Ten. *Report on Consolidation in the Financial Sector.* January 2001, pp. 147–153. Available: http://www.bis.org

[36] European Central Bank. *Mergers and Acquisitions Involving the EU Banking Industry – Facts and Implications.* December 2000, p. 21.

d) New home-markets

Access to and presence in international financial markets (e.g. the creation of new home markets) is an important opportunity offered by conglomeration across the borders of the new member states. The relevant cases of ING Group activities in Poland and Erste Bank creating new home markets in Eastern Europe are good examples of the opportunity offered by financial conglomeration to institutions. The EU banking-insurance groups increase their market shares by entering the markets of the new member states with a new customer base. The groups will have a larger customer base in new home markets and increasing possibilities for economies of scale linked to increasing revenues.[37]

e) Capital, reputation, know-how

Acquisitions in the new member states also allow the transfer of knowledge and capabilities of the EU institutions, leading to cost and revenue efficiencies in the acquired entity. A former stand-alone entity in a new member state will receive better access to capital and will enjoy the operational benefits arising from the transfer of knowledge and skills of its EU parent group. The reliance in many aspects on its EU parent group allows it to operate and grow under better conditions than its non-EU related domestic competitors.

Foreign ownership is generally seen as a stabilising factor providing expertise and increasing resources particularly in risk management and reputation. Reputation of a financial institution is mainly about ratings and the fact is that the rating of parent companies has an influence on its subsidiaries and other affiliates. Indeed, the well-known and sound EU groups as parent companies contribute to the reputation of their subsidiaries in the new member states. For example, Estonian Hansapank, the subsidiary of Swedish Foereningssparbanken–Swedbank–enjoys the good reputation of its parent group. The high ratings of Swedbank have supported that the rating of Hansapank has increased and stayed on a constant high ever since Swedbank acquired Hansapank.

f) Capacity reductions

From the banking industry perspective, conglomerations between large bank-headed groups and smaller banks seem to have been associated with capacity reductions, even though several other important factors such as business volume expansion, technological developments or changes in the

---

[37] European Central Bank. *Mergers and Acquisitions Involving the EU Banking Industry – Facts and Implications.* December 2000, p. 21.

business mix of universal banks are also relevant. Indeed, in the EU context the largest reductions in bank branches have taken place in the countries with the greatest increases in concentration in the banking sector due to M&As (such as Denmark and Sweden).[38] In the context of linkages between large EU banking-insurance groups and banking institutions in the new member states the same applies. For example, in small new member states such as the Baltic States, the number of branches of banks that have been acquired by the EU groups reduced after the acquisitions. On the other hand, cross-border mergers between sizeable institutions are believed to likely add branches to banks' network.[39]

Additionally, in the context of capacity reductions, the issue of reduction in the workforce is relevant. Usually the negative consequence of a merger is a massive layoff of workers. Massive layoff of workers is seen to constitute an integral part of each and every financial sector merger.[40] I have discussed that strategic M&A activity aims at expansion and development. Thus, the main purpose of cutting the workforce is the need for making processes more effective. Strategic expansion does not seek to cut costs as a direct objective. The issue of the layoff in the context of conglomeration linkages between the EU and the new member states is not alarming. Usually the EU financial groups operate in the new member states through separate subsidiaries and they aim to expand rather than to eliminate extra costs whenever taking their business into the new member states. Thus, the reduction in the workforce stays in reasonable limits that are necessary for effective operations.

It is likely to be the case that the capacity reductions due to the EU-initiated conglomeration activities across the new member states occur mainly because the conglomeration creates better technological and other conditions, which are necessary to deliver financial products in a more efficient manner. For example, the capacity reductions of Eesti Ühispank and Latvijas Unibanka are to a large extent driven by the changes and improvements brought about by the implementation of "e-centric vision" strategy of Skandinaviska Enskilda Banken group.

[38] European Central Bank. *Mergers and Acquisitions Involving the EU Banking Industry – Facts and Implications.* December 2000, p. 19.

[39] P. Molyneux, Y. Altunbas, E. Gardener, *Efficiency in European Banking.* John Wiley & Sons, 1996, p. 245.

[40] K. Singh, "Global Corporate Power: Emerging Trends and Issues." Asia–Pacific Journal, No. 4, June 2001.

g) Reputation risk

The major threat of financial conglomeration is reputation risk. Reputation risk is a probability that the failure of one company may lead to the declining reputation of the conglomerate as a whole. This applies to all businesses of a conglomerate. [41] For example, one part of the conglomerate (e.g., a bank in the new member state) may have to suffer and lose its clientele, with clients terminating their relationships because of mistakes or disagreements with the same clients in another part of the conglomerate (e.g., an EU bank). Similar situations can occur more often between different businesses (e.g., the banking and insurance parts of the group) in the same country.

h) "Cultural clashes" and integration difficulties

"Cultural clashes" are differences in opinion between managers of institutions with differing strategies. "Cultural clashes" may delay or hamper a smooth implementation of the expected operation. Management in one country does not have the same knowledge about the market, regulation and practice in another country. [42] One of the main threats is cultural differences between the managerial teams of the institutions involved in conglomeration. Merging the often distinct cultures of two corporate entities is a major managerial challenge, especially as differences are particularly pronounced in transactions that are across borders. In the short run, it is important to avoid the risk of disrupting and demotivating the staff and management of acquired institutions, especially in cases where the acquired institution is operating in the field of activity where the acquirer is a relatively new entrant. [43]

The challenge of responding to different corporate cultures is an issue that most institutions face due to conglomeration. The differences mainly comprise of increased risks because of different business areas, cultural barriers or other differences (unknown market, regulations, practices, etc.). Apart from explicit corporate differences and staff associating themselves with specific type of culture, there are likely to be differences in staff rules and remuneration, which can lead to friction between the

[41] European Central Bank. *Mergers and Acquisitions Involving the EU Banking Industry – Facts and Implications.* December 2000, pp. 30–31.

[42] European Central Bank. *Mergers and Acquisitions Involving the EU Banking Industry – Facts and Implications.* December 2000, pp. 23, 31.

[43] Group of Ten. *Report on Consolidation in the Financial Sector.* January 2001, pp. 147–153. Available: http://www.bis.org

two groups of personnel.[44] Due to a very different economic and political background, the new member states differ from the EU states. Thus, the institutions in the new member states are run according to local traditions and practice that certainly present a challenge for the EU financial groups. Attitude and principles at country level very often determine whether conglomeration intentions can be exercised with ease or not. A good example is the activity of Dutch Eureko B.V. in Poland. Although the Polish insurance sector has gone through extensive privatization, foreign ownership is still not completely favoured. Dutch Eureko attempted to acquire larger stakes in the largest insurance undertaking Powszechny Zaklad Ubezpieczen SA–PZU, but due to the resistance of the state, Eureko B.V. remained with 21% of the stake in PZU as its associate company.

Institutions in different countries face increased integration difficulties due to different fiscal, accounting treatment, reporting requirements etc. In addition to this, the negative impact of losing key personnel could be larger because of differences.[45]

i) Different risk management structures

From the banking industry perspective, most empirical studies on the diversification effects of mergers show that conglomeration goes hand in hand with lower individual bank risk, at least for data that are more recent. However, there are also findings that larger banks do not benefit from lower failure probabilities.[46] Apart from the beneficial diversification effect I discussed earlier conglomeration may be connected with substantial increase in risk-taking when the acquirer is entering a new market or a market that is characterised by a higher volatility of returns.

The combination of different financial activities under the same corporate roof may allow for economies of scope in the field of risk management. While the potential gains from combining portfolios with complementary exposures to risk factors can be significant, a common problem that newly created conglomerates have to confront from the beginning is how to merge together the risk control structures of the different businesses. Risk management structures inevitably reflect the realities of the

[44] European Central Bank, *Mergers and Acquisitions Involving the EU Banking Industry – Facts and Implications.* December 2000, pp. 30–31.

[45] European Central Bank, *Mergers and Acquisitions Involving the EU Banking Industry – Facts and Implications.* December 2000, pp. 30–31.

[46] E. Carletti, Ph. Hartmann, "Competition and Stability: What's Special about Banking?" European Central Bank, Working Paper No. 146, May 2002, pp. 26–27.

specific environment within which they were created and tend to differ substantially both at the conceptual and technical levels across different business lines and countries.[47]

The markets of the new member states are certainly new markets for the EU financial groups and the risk management structures of the institutions of the new member states are related to local conditions and environment. Thus, combining risk management systems in a meaningful and consistent way is a complex task that can easily be underestimated.

3.4.2. From the Perspective of Countries

At a country level, the opportunities of conglomeration can be seen in the form of benefits that the country can enjoy through conglomeration. The threats are mainly related with impact on systemic stability and supervisory issues. Financial integration in the EU and the new member states is advantageous because it increases competitiveness, leads to a more efficient financial services provision, increases the liquidity of markets and improves the development of the internal market. While the EU groups pose threats to the new member states by a too extensive expansion and the creation of dominant influence in the new member states, linkages with the new member states may create threats to the EU groups through the potential weaknesses of the legal and economic environment, and through the lesser reliability of financial systems in the new member states.

a) Strategic investment

Similar to the institution level, strategic investment is beneficial for countries. Strategic investment is direct foreign investment into the new member states and it is undertaken with long-term perspective. Strategic investment contributes to the growth and development of the financial sector of a country. The EU-initiated direct foreign investment in financial sectors of the new member states could be certainly appreciated because it does not create debt at the national level.[48] As opposed to financial investment that aims at relatively fast financial gains (and thus provides unstable funds, which might be withdrawn unexpectedly), strategic

---

[47] Group of Ten, *Report on Consolidation in the Financial Sector.* January 2001, pp. 147–153. Available: http://www.bis.org

[48] D. Gros, "Who Needs Foreign Banks?" CEPS Working Document No. 185, September 2002, p. 2.

investment provides stable funds and development expectations related to it. For example, the purchase of major stake in Hungária Biztosító RT in 1990 by Allianz AG contributed, among others, to the growth of direct foreign investment into Hungary.

b) Capital, reputation and know-how benefits

From the perspective of the new member states, financial conglomeration linkages with large EU banking-insurance groups may improve the quality of the financial sectors of the new member states. The improvement is mainly seen in capital, reputation and know-how.

Financial conglomeration means long-term foreign investment and such investment into the new member states improves their economic state. EU-linked capital contributes to the stable growth of the financial sectors of the new member states and in case of M&A activity towards some local institution it makes the financial state of the institution more stable and sound. Since EU banking-insurance groups are subject to trustworthy capital adequacy rules and supervision, the source of the capital and linkages are reliable. Thus, the new member states will be better connected to the economic area with sound financial and legal environment.

EU-linked investments into the financial sectors of a new member state create economic confidence towards the particular member state. Highly reliable regulatory and supervisory rules that apply to the EU financial institutions are translated into reliability and good reputation of the institutions. Institutions that are parts of some EU financial groups have a similarly high reputation and trust due to their linkages. As trust is the essential component of financial service provision, these institutions have a strong competitive advantage and in addition to that, they contribute to the reputation of a particular country.

EU-initiated foreign ownership in the financial sectors of the new member states usually also implies a transfer of know-how.[49] Indeed, an important issue is that in transition countries such as the new member states, the skills necessary for running a bank (or any other financial institution) existed only to a limited extent at local level. Thus, the know-how gained through conglomeration linkages with the EU banking-insurance groups contributed to the creation of skilled financial institutions in the new member states and increased the overall level of knowledge building in the financial sectors of the new member states.

[49] D. Gros, "Who Needs Foreign Banks?" CEPS Working Document No. 185, September 2002, p. 2.

c) Diversification

Financial conglomeration may enable large institutions (especially banks) to diversify risks, owing to a larger range of activities. At country level, diversification achieved through conglomeration is seen as beneficial as it can offset the systemic risk-related problems.

d) Systemic risk and the "too big to fail" issue

The major threat of financial conglomeration to countries is systemic risk and potential failures in the financial sector. Conglomeration, especially the merging of large financial institutions, has raised the issue of whether some institutions have become "too big to fail," i.e. whether the failure of a large firm may disrupt the financial system as a whole unless the authorities intervene to either keep it alive or manage its "wind-down." An additional question is whether the systemic linkages of firm failure, both domestically and internationally, have changed because of the ongoing conglomeration process. Due to disintermediation, banks can be increasingly weakened by the failure of non-banks.[50] Larger institutions engaged in a wide variety of activities become more complex to manage and monitor. In addition to that, they may become less transparent to markets and regulators.[51]

Financial stability in the EU and elsewhere in the new member states remains primarily a national concern. Conglomeration involving domestically operating financial institutions (i.e. firms whose failure may have implications for domestic systemic stability), is more of a public policy issue for national authorities than domestic firms' acquisitions of assets in other financial markets. The increase in sector consolidation has raised the issue of whether "too big to fail" concerns have increased in some countries, and, if so, what policies should be adopted to prevent or manage large failures in order to avoid systemic repercussions.[52]

In the European Union, the "too big to fail" issues arise when locally operating branches of foreign institutions are systemically more important to the host country than to the home country. For example, the failure of a member state's bank that has a branch in another smaller member state (host state) may have bigger systemic concerns in the host state

---

[50] Group of Ten, *Report on Consolidation in the Financial Sector*. January 2001, pp. 147–153. Available: http://www.bis.org

[51] European Central Bank, *Mergers and Acquisitions Involving the EU Banking Industry – Facts and Implications*. December 2000, p. 33.

[52] Group of Ten, *Report on Consolidation in the Financial Sector*. January 2001, pp. 147–153. Available: http://www.bis.org

where the branch might be large relative to the financial system and economy of the state. According to the "home country rule," it is the responsibility of a supervisory authority of the home member state to decide whether to intervene in the case of the bank's failure. Therefore, the financial stability of smaller countries may be more vulnerable to the behaviour of foreign banks, and domestic authorities may also have limited powers in the event of a systemic situation.[53] As most of the new member states are considered small relative to the 15 former EU member states, the threat of vulnerability of the new member states' financial stability certainly exists.

The principles of mutual recognition and home-country control apply to all member states of the European Union. The EU banking-insurance groups operate in the new member states mainly through subsidiaries. Those subsidiaries are subject to local supervision. Thus, the "too big to fail" issue and the potential intervention in case of systemic risk situation fall under the scope of local supervision in new member states. Considering the current situation, the issue of systemic stability is significantly important in most new member states since their financial sectors are strongly linked to the large EU banking-insurance groups. Group-level difficulties might easily turn into the difficulties of particular institutions in the new member states. In some cases the high level of integration and dominance of the EU groups in the new member states have led to such a level of market dominance that it is difficult to administer. In case the institution has significant importance at the level of a new member state, the difficulties of one institution might be translated into the difficulties of the system as a whole. The negative impact can also result from drawing out the funds and capital of a particular new member state. The situation of systemic stability may theoretically function *vice versa* when the financial institution in a new member state gets into difficulties and those difficulties are transferred to group level. However, this threat is relatively theoretical because most of the institutions in the new member states are in any case too small to affect the state of a large EU-level financial group, in spite of the linkages with the institution in difficulties.

The second policy issue is whether cross-border conglomeration will result in the emergence of pan-European institutions that are large in relation to the European financial system as a whole. The continued progress

---

[53] Group of Ten, *Report on Consolidation in the Financial Sector.* January 2001, pp. 147–153. Available: http://www.bis.org

in developing a single market for financial services in Europe results in large banks, as well as securities firms and insurance companies increasingly regarding the market at the European, rather than the national level. We have seen that the conglomeration in the EU has created some very large banking-insurance groups that might have a strong impact at the European Union level. The conglomeration that has taken place between the EU member states and relatively small new member states has created a significant influence on the local systemic concerns. Still, the establishment of linkages across new member states has not resulted in the creation of the EU-level influence.

e) Supervisory arbitrage

An increase in cross-border conglomeration involving European banks raises the issues of whether current cross-border arrangements are adequate to ensure effective co-operation and information flows between different (both bank and non-bank) supervisors, central banks and governments.[54] Financial institutions seek to take advantage of differences in rules and practices. For supervisors, the challenge lies in coping with the increased risk presented by the institutions involved in conglomeration. In cross-border conglomeration, issues of supervisory co-operation and the avoidance of undesirable supervisory arbitrage arise. Supervisory arbitrage relates, in particular, to situations involving different sectors of financial industry and jurisdictions.[55] In the European Union, the rules of minimum harmonisation of the Community legislation apply to all member states and this ensures that any sound supervisory principles commonly accepted in the European Union are followed by all member states. Thus, the issue of supervisory arbitrage would rather arise in the context of jurisdictions outside the European Union.

Since most EU banking-insurance groups operate in the new member states in the form of subsidiaries, the supervision is conducted by the "host" authority of the subsidiary, the exchange of information and allocation of responsibility in the conduct of supervision are governed by general rules. However, such important issues as crisis management, information exchange and deposit insurance are still open for finding appropriate final solutions at the European Union level.

---

[54] Group of Ten, *Report on Consolidation in the Financial Sector.* January 2001, pp. 147–153. Available: http://www.bis.org

[55] European Central Bank, *Mergers and Acquisitions Involving the EU Banking Industry – Facts and Implications.* December 2000, p. 32.

f) Neglect of SME Lending

One of the major negative fallouts of the large EU groups going across the borders of the new member states in the banking sector is the sheer neglect of lending to small and medium-sized enterprises (SMEs).[56] Large institutions standing behind local banks make it possible for local banks to finance large projects. The financing of one large project pays back more than the financing of many small business activities in terms of transaction costs *versus* revenue. Thus, the institutions with larger funding opportunities are interested in financing large projects.

Transaction costs include all costs related to an SME-loan, including salaries, advertising costs and the costs of external expertise required to evaluate the collateral. Usually the reason why banks might be reluctant to grant a loan due to transaction costs is the loan amount. The usual rule for the estimation of transaction costs related to an SME-loan is simple— the smaller the loan, the higher the transaction costs of the loan. The cost of risk analysis is assumed too high in the case of SME loans and SME finance by nature is often considered an unprofitable segment of a bank's activity.[57] When taking into consideration the European SME-definition,[58] one can conclude that most of the businesses in the new member states are SMEs. Particularly in countries where SMEs constitute the backbone of manufacturing and services sector, the consequences for the real economy could be incredibly difficult.

g) Adapting to single currency

The introduction of the euro might create difficulties for local institutions to adapt to it. As the EU financial groups acquire important posi-

---

[56] Group of Ten, *Report on Consolidation in the Financial Sector. January 2001*, pp. 147–153. Available: http://www.bis.org

[57] I. Ulst, R. Raa, "Basel II and Lending to SMEs: What Lies Ahead?" Estonian Business School, EBS Review No 16, July 2003, pp. 64–65.

[58] The European Commission (in its Recommendation 2003/361/EC) defines SMEs as enterprises with less than 250 employees and with either a maximum annual turnover of EUR 50 million or an annual balance sheet total not exceeding EUR 43 million. They also have to conform to the criterion of independence: those enterprises, which are not owned as to 25% or more of the capital or the voting rights by one enterprise, or jointly by several enterprises falling outside the definition of an SME. A small enterprise has fewer than 50 employees and reaches either a maximum annual turnover of EUR 10 million or a maximum annual balance sheet total of EUR 10 million. The micro-enterprise is further distinguished from other small enterprises as an enterprise with less than 10 employees and with either a maximum annual turnover of EUR 2 million or an annual balance sheet total not exceeding EUR 2 million.

tions in the new member states, the local financial institutions find themselves under strong pressure. Institutions that are big by local standards and have a strong niche in their national currency-denominated markets but are small by European standards, could be badly placed to cope with changes brought about by the introduction of euro and be forced to adjust. The intra-EU Merita-Nordbanken merger of the largest Finnish bank with the third largest Swedish institution is an obvious example of the sort of response that can take place.[59]

[59] D. Mayes, J. Vesala, "On the Problems of Home Country Control." Bank of Finland Discussion Papers 20/98, 1998, p. 10.

Conclusion

This book discussed the nature, benefits and risks of financial conglomeration. It also studied the banking-insurance conglomerates in the EU, determined their linkages with the new member states and impact on the new member states. The book looked at the developments of financial conglomeration in the EU and covered financial conglomeration linkages between the EU and the new member states. I examined a few cases of the creation of linkages between the EU banking-insurance groups and institutions in the new member states. Finally the book addressed the implications of financial conglomeration across the new member states, highlighting the major opportunities and threats of financial conglomeration.

Main Findings on Chapter 1
Financial conglomerates comprise of financial and non-financial enterprises that have formed a specific group structure. When the structure and other elements of a group are in accordance with the European Union conglomeration criteria, the group is deemed to be a financial conglomerate and subject to supplementary supervision of financial conglomerates. According to the European Union legislation, the existence of an insurance undertaking in a group is a compulsory element when identifying financial conglomerates. Usually financial conglomerates comprise of credit institutions and insurance undertakings, one of them (usually a bank) being the head of the group.

Financial conglomeration is seen as beneficial by the institutions because it allows cost efficiencies and revenue efficiencies (in both cases through economies of scale and scope), diversification and lower risk benefits, informational advantages and market power. The external driving forces of financial conglomeration are improvements in information technology, government policies, deregulation and globalisation of marketplace. Although beneficial in many aspects, financial conglomeration is linked to several problems. The major risks and potential problems of conglomeration are regulatory arbitrage, internal contagion effects, complexity and lack of transparency effects, conflicts of interest, market concentration and reduction of competition, and the issue of unregulated entities. The rules on capital adequacy and supervision, the constant monitoring of the activities of a group, transparency requirements, exchange of information and co-operation between supervisory authorities present the most important safeguards against the risks and problems of financial conglomeration.

Main Findings on Chapter 2
The book provided a survey on banking and insurance undertakings both in the EU and the new member states, in order to examine the degree of financial conglomeration across these institutions. The book also aimed at analysing the strategies used by some important EU banking-insurance conglomerates in their activities across the financial sectors of the new member states and defining the reasons of bank/insurance mergers into the new member states.

The analysis on the EU banking sector allows the conclusion to be drawn that the largest banks and banking groups present a significant market power at the level of their home countries. A relatively large part of assets of important EU banking institutions is concentrated in a few countries and their extremely large institutions—the "big players." The largest banks in the EU have grown significantly due to M&A transactions, the largest of which have been concluded mostly between the entities belonging to the same nationality. Most of the largest EU banks and insurance firms are related to other corresponding sector and thus form parts of banking-insurance groups in the EU. The largest banks are mainly in the centre of groups. The insurance activities of banks are often conducted in the form of bancassurance—a package of financial services that can fulfil both banking and insurance needs at the same time.

The results of the survey on cross-sector M&A activities in the EU allow the conclusion that the most important deals (e.g., Allianz AG's acquisition of Dresdner Bank AG) have been domestic deals. Domestic deals with bank as an acquirer and insurance firm as a target are the dominant form of M&A activities between the EU banks and insurance firms.

When it comes to the identification of the significance of EU banking-insurance groups, the asset-base of the groups is remarkable. Most of the EU banking-insurance groups can (and evidently will) be considered important "players" in the financial services provision both at their domestic and the EU-level. Thus, most of the defined banking-insurance groups will probably become subject to the supplementary supervision regime of financial conglomerates.

Main Findings on Chapter 3

Financial sectors of the new member states have high bank dominance. The survey on banking sectors of the new member states reflects that the EU-linked consolidation is strongest in Estonia. The market shares of the EU-linked banks are also relatively high in Lithuania, Slovakia and the Czech Republic. This indicates that the countries will be strongly influenced by the changes in the relevant EU banking-insurance groups and the EU financial sector in general. *Vice versa*, the changes in the EU-linked banks and financial sectors in the new member states might be transferred to the linked EU institutions.

The analysis on the insurance sectors of the new member states allows the conclusion that the insurance markets in the new member states are relatively concentrated and divided among larger "players." Compared to the relatively strong EU banking-insurance linkages of largest banks, large insurance providers of the new member states are significantly less EU-linked. The survey suggests that Hungary and Estonia have clear dominance of the EU-linked undertakings in terms of market share, while Cyprus and Slovenia have no EU-linked undertakings among the five largest insurance providers.

The analysis on the linkages between the EU groups and institutions in the new member states allows the conclusion that many large EU banking-insurance groups have significant business undertakings in the new member states. Banking sectors of the new member states are particularly strongly EU-related and dominated by banks belonging to some large EU banking-insurance group. Examination of the significance of the EU-linkages results in the conclusion that in addition to relatively strong connections, the related entities are generally important "players" in the new member states. This applies particularly to the banking sector that forms the dominant part of the financial sector in all the new member states. Larger new member states have connections with more EU countries than smaller new member states because larger markets are more attractive and allow the presence of more players. The survey shows that the Continental European groups have presence in East and Central European new member states while Scandinavian groups have strong preference in the Baltic

States. The analysis allows us to draw the conclusion that besides institution-specific factors, country-specific factors have played a certain role in the expansion into the new member states. The new member states have been, currently are and will be an attractive investment area for the EU banking-insurance groups.

The result of M&As in the banking industry in Central and Eastern Europe is that most domestic banks have become subsidiaries of large foreign groups. In the wake of massive privatisation programs, foreign banks have rapidly taken control over the domestic banking industry in this region. The most common form of the EU banking and insurance groups' business expansion into the new member states has been M&A activities that have generally followed two patterns. On one hand, the advantageous market conditions and favourable legislative/administrative situations in the new member states have increased the interest of the EU groups in the new member states and the attractiveness of institutions of the new member states. On the other hand, general M&A trends in Europe and in the world have also influenced M&A activities in the new member states. Increased activity of M&As in the new member states coincides with the trend of world-wide M&A activities.

In order to determine some M&A criteria of the EU groups across the new member states and discuss what the main ideas behind the acquisitions might have been, the book briefly looked at the most important M&A business transactions of four EU banking-insurance groups. The short case studies examined four successful M&A strategies—those of Erste Bank, ING Group, Skandinaviska Enskilda Banken and Allianz AG. The case studies addressed the related acquisitions of Ceska Sporitelna and Slovenská Sporitelna; Bank Slaski w Katowicach; Eesti Ühispank, Latvijas Unibanka and Vilniaus Bankas; and Hungária Biztosító RT.

Erste Bank's strategies in the Czech Republic and Slovakia were based on the difference in business sector orientation and aimed at building a retail network. ING Group aimed at the creation of a new home market in Poland, with the strong country focus being based on the expectations of a significant growth of the market share, an improvement of competitive edge and global brand building. Skandinaviska Enskilda Banken expanded successfully with "e-centric" vision into the Baltic States, while Allianz AG enjoyed the benefits of liberalisation of emerging economies in Hungary.

Financial conglomeration across the new member states has implications for both the institutions and the countries. From the perspective of institutions, the main opportunities of financial conglomeration are potential benefits from strategic investment; diversification; cost and revenue benefits; creation of new home-markets; access to capital, reputation and know-how and possible capacity reductions. The major threat of financial conglomeration is reputation risk; institutions may also face "cultural clashes," integration difficulties and a difference in risk management structures.

From the perspective of countries, the opportunities of conglomeration appear in the form of benefits the country can enjoy through conglomeration. The major opportunities of financial conglomeration for the countries are the benefits of strategic investment; capital, reputation and know-how benefits; and diversification that can offset the systemic risk-related problems.

The major threats of financial conglomeration to the countries are systemic risk and potential failures in the financial sector. While the new member states face a too extensive expansion and the creation of dominant influence by the large EU groups, linkages with the new member states might create threats to the EU groups through potential weaknesses of the legal and economic environment, and lesser soundness of financial systems in the new member states. Conglomeration has raised the main issue of systemic concern: whether some or more institutions have become "too big to fail." The second issue of systemic concern is whether cross-border conglomeration will result in the emergence of pan-European institutions that are large in relation to the European financial system as a whole. From the perspective of supervisors, a threat of supervisory arbitrage should be taken into consideration because financial institutions seek to take advantage of differences in rules and practices. Since the new member states have implemented the minimum prudential legislation similar to the 15 former member states, supervisory arbitrage is more likely the case when it concerns the jurisdictions outside the European Union.

From the perspective of countries, another negative aspect about large EU financial institutions going across the banking sectors of the new member states is the neglect of lending to SMEs. Particularly in countries, where SMEs constitute the backbone of the manufacturing and services sector, the consequences for the real economy could be incredibly difficult. And last but not least—in the context of the introduction of the euro-countries recognise that local institutions may face difficulties with adapting to a single currency.

Abbreviations

AT	Austria
BE	Belgium
CZ	The Czech Republic
CY	Cyprus
DE	Germany
DK	Denmark
EE	Estonia
ES	Spain
EU	The European Union
FI	Finland
FR	France
GB	The United Kingdom
GR	Greece
HU	Hungary
IE	Ireland
IT	Italy
LT	Lithuania
LV	Latvia
LU	Luxembourg
MT	Malta
NL	The Netherlands
NO	Norway
PL	Poland
PT	Portugal
SE	Sweden
SK	Slovakia
SL	Slovenia
UK	The United Kingdom
US	The United States of America

References

7th *Directive 83/349/EEC of 13 June 1983 based on the Article 54 (3) (g) of the Treaty on Consolidated Accounts.* OJ L193, 18 July 1983, pp. 001–0017.

Balcerowicz, L. *Towards Integration: Evolution of the Financial System of the New Member States and Their Integration with the EU Financial System.* Centre for Financial Studies, Colloquium: Globalisation of Financial Markets—Risks and Opportunities, Frankfurt, March 2003.

Berger, A. N., R. De Young, H. Genay and G. F. Udell. *Globalisation of Financial Institutions: Evidence from Cross-Border Banking Performance.* Brookings-Wharton Papers on Financial Services, 2000, Vol. 3, pp. 6, 12–14.

Boyd, J. and S. Graham. "The Profitability and Risk Effects of Allowing Bank Holding Companies to Merge with Other Financial Firms." *Federal Reserve Bank of Minneapolis, Quarterly Review,* 1998, pp. 3–20.

Brealey, R. A. and S. C. Myers. *Principles of Corporate Finance.* McGraw-Hill Companies, New York, 2003, pp. 931–932.

Buch, C. M. *Why Do Banks Go Abroad? – Evidence from German Data.* Kiel Working Paper No. 948, p. 8.

Buch, C. M. and G. L. DeLong. *Cross-Border Bank Mergers: What Lures the Rare Animal?* Kiel Working Paper No. 1070, August 2001, p. 9.

Cabral, I., F. Dierick, F. and J. Vesala. *Banking Integration in the Euro Area.* European Central Bank, Occasional Paper No. 6, December 2002, p. 42.

Carletti, E. and Ph. Hartmann. *Competition and Stability: What's Special About Banking?* European Central Bank, Working Paper No. 146, May 2002, pp. 26–27.

Claessens, S. *Benefits and Costs of Integrated Financial Services Provision in Developing Countries.* University of Amsterdam and CEPR, 14 November 2002, pp. 7, 13–16, 18–21, 25– 27, 30.

Comité Européen des Assurances. European Insurance in Figures. Complete Data 2001.

Cranston, R. *Principles of Banking Law.* Oxford University Press, 1997, pp. 38–39.

Czech National Bank, National Bank of Hungary, National Bank of Poland, National Bank of Slovakia, Bank of Slovenia. Stability and Structure of Financial Systems in CEC5. Warsaw, May 2002, pp. 9–27, 34–46.

De Larosière, J. and E. Barthalon. *Banking Consolidation in Europe: Adapting to Financial Consolidation.* Routledge International Studies in Money and Banking, 2001, pp. 15–16.

De Nicolo, G. *Consolidation, Conglomeration and Financial Risk: A Progress Report.* International Monetary Fund, Mae Department, Presentation, July 2002.

Dermin, J. *European Banking: Past, Present and Future.* Conference Paper for the Second ECB Central Banking Conference, Frankfurt am Main, 24 and 25 October 2002, pp. 27–29.

Directive 2002/87/EC of the European Parliament and of the Council of 16 December 2002 on the supplementary supervision of credit institutions, insurance undertakings and investment firms in a financial conglomerate and amending Council Directives 73/239/EEC, 79/267/EEC, 92/49/EEC, 92/96/EEC, 93/6/EEC and 93/22/EEC, and Directives 98/78/EC and 2000/12/EC of the European Parliament and of the Council. OJ L035, 11 February 2003, pp. 001–0027.

Eatwell, J. and L. Taylor. *Global Finance at Risk: The Case for International Regulation.* Polity Press, 2000, p. 199.

Eppendorfer, C., R. Beckmann and M. Neimke. *Market Access Strategies in the EU Banking Sector: Obstacles and Benefits Towards an Integrated European Retail Market.* January 2002, pp. 3–5, 10–11.

European Central Bank. Banking in the Euro Area: Structural Features and Trends. April 1999, pp. 46–48.

European Central Bank. EU Banking Sector Stability. February 2003, pp. 13, 16–17, 20.

European Central Bank. EU Bank's Income Structure. Monthly Bulletin, April 2000, p. 7.

European Central Bank. Mergers and Acquisitions Involving the EU Banking Industry— Facts and Implications. December 2000, pp. 13, 15, 19–23, 30–33.

European Central Bank. The Effects of Technology on the EU Banking System. July 1999, p. 31.

European Commission. Enlargement Papers. Update of the Report on Macroeconomic and Financial Sector Stability Developments in Candidate Countries. European Economy, No. 11, November 2002.

European Commission. Recommendation 2003/361/EC of 6 May 2003 concerning the definition of micro, small and medium-sized enterprises. OJL 124, 20 May 2003, pp. 0036–0041.

European Commission. Enlargement Directorate-General. Enlargement of the European Union: An Historic Opportunity, Brussels, May 2003.

European Commission. Internal Market Directorate General. Towards an EU Directive on the Prudential Supervision of Financial Conglomerates: Consultation Document. MARKT/3021/00-EN, 2000, pp. 5, 13, 24.

Federal Reserve System of the U.S. To What Extent Will the Banking Industry Be Globalised? A Study of Bank Nationality and Reach in 20 European Nations. International Finance Discussion Papers, No. 725, May 2002. Available: http://www.federalreserve.gov/pubs/ifdp (last visited in May 2003).

Focarelli, D., F. Panetta, F. and C. Salleo. "Why Do Banks Merge?" *Journal of Money, Credit and Banking,* October 2000, pp. 13–14.

Focarelli, D. and A. F. Pozzolo. *The Determinants of Cross-Border Bank Shareholdings: An Analysis with Bank-Level Data from OECD Countries.* Banca d'Italia, Temi di discussione del Servizio Studi, No. 381, October 2000, pp. 13–14.

Foster Reed, S. and A. Reed Lajoux. *The Art of M&A: A Merger/Acquisition/Buyout Guide.* McGraw-Hill Companies, New York, 1998, pp. 15, 27, 921.

Freedman, S.R. *Regulating the Modern Financial Firm: Implications of Disintermediation and Conglomeration.* University of St. Gallen, Discussion Paper No. 2000-21, September 2000, pp. 15, 20.

Gros, D. *Who Needs Foreign Banks?* CEPS Working Document No. 185, September 2002, p. 2.

Group of Ten. *Report on Consolidation in the Financial Sector.* January 2001, pp. 47–54, 65–73, 147–153. Available: http://www.bis.org/publ/gten05.pdf (last visited in August 2003).

Gruson, M. *Supervision of Financial Holding Companies in Europe: The Proposed EU Directive on Supplementary Supervision of Financial Conglomerates.* J.W. Goethe University, Institut für Bankrecht, Working Paper No. 94, 2001, pp. 16–17, 21–22.

Half, C. *Evolving Trends in the Supervision of Financial Conglomerates: A Comparative Investigation of Responses to the Challenges of Cross-Sectoral Supervision in the United States, European Union, and United Kingdom.* Harvard Law School: International Finance Seminar, 30 April 2002, pp. 5–6, 15, 28.

ING Bank Slaski SA. Annual Report, 2001. Available: http//www.ing.pl (last visited in July 2003).

ING Bank Slaski SA. Annual Report, 2002. Available: http//www.ing.pl (last visited in July 2003).

Jackson, H.E. and C. Half. *Background Paper on Evolving Trends in the Supervision of Financial Conglomerates.* Conference Paper, 26 June 2002, pp. 8–9, 15–18.

Kumar, M. *Bancassurance. Financial Express,* 11 April 2000. Available: http://www.einsurance professional.com/artbuzz.htm (last visited in June 2003).

Kuritzkes, A., T. Schuermann and S. M. Weiner. *Risk Measurement, Risk Management and Capital Adequacy in Financial Conglomerates.* The Wharton Financial Institutions Centre, 2002, pp. 13–14.

Leach, A. *European Bancassurance.* Financial Times, London, 1993.

Lipton, M. *Mergers: Past, Present and Future.* Wachtell, Lipton, Rosen & Katz, 10 January 2001.

Mankiw, N.G. *Principles of Economics.* Harcourt College Publishers, 2001, p. 813.

Mayes, D. and J. Vesala. *On the Problems of Home Country Control.* Bank of Finland Discussion Papers, No. 20/98, 1998, p. 10.

Mediobanca R&S. Largest European Banks: Financial Aggregates, 2002, pp. 5–9. Available: http://www.mbres.it (last visited in May 2003).

Molyneux, P., Y. Altunbas and E. Gardener. *Efficiency in European Banking.* John Wiley & Sons, 1996, pp. 32, 49, 223, 245.

Morrison, A.D. *The Economics of Capital Regulation in Financial Conglomerates.* Merton College and Said Business School, University of Oxford, August 2002, p. 4.

National Bank of Belgium. Financial Conglomerates. Financial Stability Review, 2002, pp. 61–64, 68–70, 74–75.

Reed Lajoux, A. and J. F. Weston. *The Art of M&A Financing and Refinancing: A Guide to Sources and Instruments of External Growth.* McGraw-Hill Companies, New York, 1999, pp. 296–298.

Sanchez Peinado, E. *Internationalisation Process of Spanish Banks: A New Stage After the Mergers.* University of Valencia, Faculty of Economics, 2001.

Santomero, A.M. and E. J. Chung. *Evidence in Support of Broader Bank Powers. Financial Markets, Institutions and Instruments*, New York University, Salomon Centre, 1992, pp. 1–69.

Shull, B. and L. J. White. "The Right Corporate Structure for Expanded Bank Activities." *The Banking Law Journal*, No. 4, May 1998, p. 474.

Singh, K. "Global Corporate Power: Emerging Trends and Issues." *Asia-Pacific Journal*, No. 4, June 2001.

Skandinaviska Enskilda Banken. Annual Report, 1998. Available: http://taz.vv.sebank.se/ (last visited in July 2003).

Skipper Jr., H.D. *Financial Services Integration Worldwide: Promises and Pitfalls*. Georgia State University, 2000, pp. 3–11, 43–48. Available: http://www.worldbank.org/wbi/banking/insurance/contractual/pdf/skipper.pdf (last visited in June 2003).

Smid, S. and S. Noordam. *Financial Services on Malta: Study on the Situation of Enterprises, the Industry and the Service Sectors in Turkey, Cyprus and on Malta*. December 2002, p. 6.

Ulst, I. and R. Raa. "Basel II and Lending to SMEs: What Lies Ahead?" *Estonian Business School, EBS Review*, No 16, July 2003, pp. 64–65.

United Nations Conference on Trade and Development. Handbook of Statistics, International Finance: Foreign Direct Investment. Available: http://stats.unctad.org (last visited in August 2003).

Van Lelyveld, I. and A. Schilder. *Risk in Financial Conglomerates: Management and Supervision. Joint US–Netherlands Roundtable on Financial Services Conglomerates*, Washington D.C., November 2002, Research Series Supervision, No. 49, pp. 5–6, 9–11.

Vander Vennet, R. "Cost and Profit Efficiency of Financial Conglomerates and Universal Banks in Europe." *Journal of Money, Credit and Banking*, Vol. 34/1, February 2002, pp. 260, 279.

Sources of Research Data

Internet Sources[1]

Abanka Vipa DD, http://www.abanka.si (last visited in July 2003)
ABN Amro NV, http://www.abnamro.com (last visited in June 2003)
Aegon NV, http://www.aegon.com (last visited in June 2003)
AG Balta, http://www.balta.lv (last visited in July 2003)
Allianz AG, http://www.allianz.com (last visited in August 2003)
Alpha Bank Ltd, http://www.alphabank.com.cy (last visited in July 2003)
APS Bank Ltd, http://www.apsbank.com.mt (last visited in July 2003)
Association of Austrian Insurance Companies, http://www.vvo.at (last visited in June 2003)
Association of Banks (Slovakia), http://www.asocbank.sk (last visited in July 2003)
Association of Cyprus Commercial Banks, http://www.accb.com.cy (last visited in July 2003)
Association of German Banks, http://www.german-banks.com (last visited in July 2003)
Association of Hungarian Insurance Companies, http://www.mabisz.hu (last visited in July 2003)
Association of Insurance Companies-Greece, http://www.eaee.gr (last visited in June 2003)
Association of Latvian Commercial Banks, http://eng.bankasoc.lv (last visited in July 2003)
Austrian Bankers' Association, http://www.voebb.at (last visited in June 2003)
Banca Intesa Spa, http://www.bancaintesa.it (last visited in June 2003)
Banca Nazionale del Lavoro, http://www.bnl.it (last visited in June 2003)
Bank of Lithuania, http://www.lb.lt (last visited in July 2003)
Bank of Slovenia, http://www.bsi.si (last visited in July 2003)
Bank of Valletta Plc, http://www.bov.com (last visited in July 2003)
Bank Przemyslowo-Handlowy–BPK, http://www.bph.pl (last visited in July 2003)
Banka Koper DD, http://www.banka-koper.si (last visited in July 2003)
Bankas Snoras, http://www.snoras.com (last visited in July 2003)
Barclays Plc, http://www.barclays.com (last visited in June 2003)

---

[1] The information in brackets refers to the dates the author last visited the websites.

Belgian Bankers' Association, http://www.abb-bvb.be (last visited in July 2003)
BNP Paribas, http://www.bnpparibas.com (last visited in June 2003)
British Bankers' Association, http://www.bba.org.uk (last visited in July 2003)
Bundesverband Deutscher Banken, http://www.bdb.de (last visited in August 2003)
Central Bank of Ireland, http://www.centralbank.ie (last visited in July 2003)
Ceska Pojistovna AS, http://www.cpoj.cz (last visited in July 2003)
Ceska Sporitelna AS, http://www.csas.cz; (last visited in July 2003)
Ceskoslovenska Obchodni Banka, http://www.csob.cz (last visited in July 2003)
Citibank (Poland), http://www.citibank.pl (last visited in July 2003)
Comité Européen des Assurances, http://www.cea.assur.org (last visited in August 2003)
Credit Lyonnais, http://www.creditlyonnais.com (last visited in June 2003)
Czech Banking Association, http://www.czech-ba.cz (last visited in July 2003)
Czech Insurance Association, http://www.cap.cz (last visited in July 2003)
Czech National Bank, http://www.cnb.cz (last visited in July 2003)
Cyprus Popular Bank Ltd–Laiki Bank, http://www.laiki.com (last visited in July 2003)
Danish Bankers' Association, http://www.finansraadet.dk (last visited in June 2003)
Deutsche Bank AG, http://www.db.com (last visited in June 2003)
Drauda, http://www.drauda.lt (last visited in July 2003)
DZ-Bank AG, http://www.dzbank.de (last visited in June 2003)
ERGO Kindlustuse AS, http://www.ergo-kindlustus.ee (last visited in July 2003)
Ergo Lietuva, http://www.ergo.lt (last visited in July 2003)
Erste Bank Group, http://www.sparkasse.at/erstebank/group/home (last visited in August 2003)
Estonian Banking Association, http://www.pangaliit.ee (last visited in July 2003)
Estonian Insurers' Association, http://www.eksl.ee (last visited in July 2003)
Eureko BV, http://www.eureko.net (last visited in July 2003)
Eurolife, http://www.eurolife.com.cy (last visited in July 2003)
European Banking Federation, http://www.fbe.be (last visited in July 2003)
Federation of Finnish Insurance Companies, http://www.vakes.fi (last visited in June 2003)
Finantsinspektsioon – Financial Supervision Authority, http://www.fi.ee (last visited in July 2003)
Finnish Bankers' Association, http://www.pankkiyhdistys.fi (last visited in June 2003)
Foereningssparbanken–Swedbank, http://www.foreningssparbanken.se (last visited in July 2003)
Forsikring & Pension, http://www.forsikringenshus.dk (last visited in June 2003)
French Bankers Association, http://www.fbf.fr (last visited in June 2003)
French Federation of Insurance Companies, http://www.ffsa.fr (last visited in June 2003)
GE Capital Bank AS, http://www.gecapital.cz (last visited in July 2003)
Generali Group, http://www.generali.com (last visited in June 2003)
German Insurance Industry Association, http://www.gdv.de (last visited in June 2003)
Groupe Banques Populaires, http://www.banquepopulaire.fr (last visited in July 2003)
Groupe Société Générale, http://www.socgen.com (last visited in August 2003)
Hansapank, http://www.hansa.ee (last visited in August 2003)
HBOS Plc, http://www.hbosplc.com (last visited in June 2003)
Hellenic Bank Ltd, http://www.hellenicbank.com (last visited in July 2003)

Hellenic Bank Association, http://www.hba.gr (last visited in June 2003)
HSBC Bank Malta Plc, http://www.hsbc.com.mt (last visited in July 2003)
Hungarian Banking Association, http://www.bankszovetseg.hu/magunkrol_en.html (last visited in July 2003)
HVB Bank Czech Republic AS, http://www.hvb.cz (last visited in July 2003)
HVB Bank Slovakia, http://www.baca.sk (last visited in July 2003)
HVB Group, http://www.hvbgroup.com (last visited in August 2003)
If Draudimas, http://www.if.lt (last visited in July 2003)
If-Eesti Kindlustus AS, http://www.if.ee/et/index.asp (last visited in July 2003)
ING Group, http://www.ing.com (last visited in July 2003)
Insurance Association of Cyprus, http://www.iac.org.cy (last visited in July 2003)
Insurance Information Institute, http://www.internationalinsurance.org/default.htm (last visited in July 2003)
Irish Bankers' Federation, http://www.ibis.ie (last visited in June 2003)
Italian Banking Association, http://www.abi.it (last visited in June 2003)
KBC Bank and Insurance Group, http://www.kbc.com (last visited in August 2003)
Komercni Banka, http://www.kb.cz (last visited in July 2003)
Komisja Nadzoru Ubezpieczen i Funduszy Emerytalnych, http://www.knuife.gov.pl (last visited in July 2003)
Latvian Insurers Association, http://www.laa.lv (last visited in July 2003)
Lietuvos Draudimas, http://www.ldr.lt (last visited in July 2003)
Lietuvos Z.U. Bankas, http://www.lzub.lt (last visited in July 2003)
Luxembourg Bankers' Association, http://www.abbl.lu (last visited in June 2003)
Malta Financial Services Authority, http://www.mfsa.com.mt (last visited in July 2003)
National Association of Insurance Companies, http://www.ania.it (last visited in June 2003)
National Bank of Poland, http://www.nbp.pl (last visited in July 2003)
Nordea AB, http://www.nordea.com (last visited in August 2003)
Nova Ljubljanska Banka, http://www.nlb.si (last visited in July 2003)
Parex Bank, http://www.parex.net (last visited in July 2003)
Polish Bank Association, http://www.zbp.pl (last visited in July 2003)
Powszechny Zaklad Ubezpieczen SA-PZU, http://www.pzuzycie.com.pl (last visited in July 2003)
Preventa, http://www.preventa.lt (last visited in July 2003)
Professional Union of Insurance Companies (UPEA), http://www.bvvo.be (last visited in June 2003)
Rietumu Bank Group, http://www.rietumu.lv (last visited in July 2003)
Sampo Group, http://www.sampo.com (last visited in August 2003)
SEB Group, http://www.seb.net (last visited in August 2003)
Seesam International Insurance, http://www.seesam.ee (last visited in July 2003)
Slovenian Insurance Association, http://www.zav-zdruzenje.si (last visited in July 2003)
Slovenska Sporitelna, http://www.slsp.sk (last visited in July 2003)
Spanish Bankers' Association, http://www.aebanca.com (last visited in June 2003)
Spanish Union of Insurance and Reinsurance Companies, http://www.unespa.es (last visited in June 2003)
Swedish Bankers' Association, http://www.bankforeningen.se (last visited in June 2003)

Swedish Insurance Federation (http://www.forsakringsforbundet.com (last visited in June 2003)

Tatra Banka AS, http://www.tatrabanka.sk (last visited in July 2003)

The Bank Association of Slovenia, http://www.zbs-giz.si (last visited in July 2003)

The British Insurers' European Committee, http://www.abi.org.uk (last visited in June 2003)

The Financial Market Authority (Slovakia), http://www.uft.sk/en/insurance (last visited in July 2003)

The Irish Insurance Federation, http://www.iif.ie (last visited in June 2003)

The Netherlands Bankers' Association, http://www.nvb.nl (last visited in June 2003)

The Polish Chamber of Insurance, http://www.piu.org.pl (last visited in July 2003)

The Royal Bank of Scotland, http://www.royalbankscot.co.uk (last visited in June 2003)

TuIR Warta SA, http://www.warta.pl (last visited in July 2003)

Ukio Bankas, http://www.ub.lt/lt (last visited in July 2003)

Unibanka AS, http://www.unibanka.sk (last visited in July 2003)

Verbond van Verzekeraars in Nederland, http://www.verzekeraars.nl (last visited in June 2003)

Databases

Bureau van Dijk Electronic Publishing. BankScope, global bank database.

Bureau van Dijk Electronic Publishing. ISIS, insurance information and statistics.

FactSet Mergerstat Llc. Mergerstat, global mergers and acquisitions information.

Reed Elsevier Plc, LexisNexis Group. LexisNexis for law, public records, company data, government, academic and business news source. Available: http://www.lexis-nexis.com/professional.

Thomson Financial. Securities Data Company (SDC) Platinum, financial transactions database.

Thomson Financial. Thomson Extel Cards Database.

Index

allfinanz, 12
asset management, 12, 15, 25, 67
asset-base, 60, 67, 118
associate company, 88, 109

bancassurance, 12, 15, 21,30, 57, 60, 65, 72, 104, 118
    bancassurance group, 60
        See also banking-insurance group
bank, 2–15, 21–35, 41–53, 73–109, 112–120
    commercial bank, 10, 18, 41, 52, 71, 77
    co-operative bank, 15, 41, 45, 49, 52
    mortgage bank, 41
    mutual bank, 15
    savings bank, 41, 45, 52, 96
    special purpose bank, 41
    specialised bank, 15, 19
    universal bank, 10, 15, 71, 107
    universal bank model, 9
    universal bank structure, 9
bank dominance, 71, 119
banking, 2–22, 41, 57–61, 67–87, 90–94, 108, 118
    banking activity, 19
    banking business, 24, 41, 53, 57, 76–77
    banking group, 15, 41–53, 73–84, 96, 102, 118–120
    banking industry, 12–14, 24, 61, 90, 102, 120
        See also financial industry
    banking intermediation, 19
    banking market, 47, 71–78, 90, 98–99
    banking sector, 12, 41–53, 65–73, 82–84, 96, 107–121
        See also financial sector
    banking structure, 41, 45
    banking system, 48
    banking-insurance group, 2–4, 45, 59–97, 104–120

commercial banking, 15, 20
    investment banking, 10, 15, 26
    retail banking, 96, 103
    universal banking, 14, 15, 41, 71, 100
block-holder, 12
branch, 13, 77, 107, 112–113
    branch network, 27
brokerage, 8

capital market, 11–12, 67
casualty insurance, 22
commercial alliance, 52
competition, 1, 12, 17–19, 23–27, 32, 38, 82, 98
    fair competition, 26
    inter-sector competition, 25
    intra-sector competition, 25
conflict of interest, 20, 26, 32, 38, 118
conglomerate, 7–19, 22, 29–39, 65, 103–109
    banking-insurance conglomerate, 2, 117–118
        See also financial conglomerate *and* financial group
    conglomerate formation, 14
    conglomerate structure, 4, 9, 10, 33–34
    general conglomerate, 11–12, 16, 34
    universal banking conglomerate, 10
conglomeration, 1–17, 23–38, 102–121
    banking-insurance conglomeration, 1–4, 58
        See also financial conglomeration
    cross-border conglomeration, 113–114, 121
consolidation, 1, 12–27, 72–79, 90, 98–99, 112, 119
    banking-insurance consolidation, 2
    cross-border consolidation, 1
    financial consolidation, 1, 69
controlling interest, 86
corporate governance, 11
    corporate governance arrangement, 12
cost, 12–13, 16–17
    computing cost, 28
    cost advantage, 18, 29
    cost benefit, 105, 121
    cost effect, 29
    cost of information technology, 25, 29
    cost of production, 29, 38
    cost reduction, 100, 101
    cost saving, 23, 25
    fixed cost, 24, 28–29
    information cost, 23, 25, 30

monitoring cost, 23, 30
    operating cost, 28
    overhead cost, 29
    social cost, 26–27
    transaction cost, 25, 30, 115
    transportation cost, 13
credit institution, 8, 41, 65, 71, 77, 95, 117
crisis management, 58, 114
cross-border activity, 13
    See also cross-border mergers & acquisitions (M&A) activity
cross-border capital controls, 11
cross-border expansion, 4, 89
cross-marketing, 30
cross-sector conglomeration deal, 65
cross-sector deal value, 65
cross-sector transaction, 67
cross-selling, 19–20, 98, 105
cultural clashes, 108, 121

deregulation, 1, 11–15, 23–28, 117
disclosure, 37
    disclosure rules, 38
diversification, 7, 9, 16–24, 98, 103–121
    diversification advantage, 35
    diversification benefit, 11, 22, 35
    diversification effect, 109
    diversification gain, 18
    product diversification, 21
diversified business, 16
domestic capital, 73

e-centric approach, 100
economy of scale, 1, 16–29, 89, 106, 117
    cost-based economy of scale, 17
    revenue-based economy of scale, 19, 21
economy of scope, 16–21, 29–30, 67, 109, 117
    cost-based economy of scope, 17
    revenue-based economy of scope, 19–20
effects of scale, 98
efficiency, 12, 17–19, 27–29, 99–100
    capital market efficiency, 11
    cost efficiency, 17–19, 29, 106, 117
    operational efficiency, 16, 29
    universal banking efficiency, 18
entity, 9
    corporate entity, 9

financial sector entity, 10–11
legal entity, 9
non-regulated entity, 8, 10
regulated entity, 8, 33–34, 36
unregulated entity, 9, 32, 39, 40, 118
excessive leverage, 32–33, 39

financial activity, 8–10, 86, 109
See also banking activity *and* insurance activity
cross-sector financial activity, 10
financial business, 3, 86–87
See also banking business *and* insurance business
financial company, 7
See also insurance company
financial conglomerate, 2, 8–41, 68–69, 117–119
See also banking-insurance conglomerate *and* financial group
formation of financial conglomerates, 65
financial conglomeration, 1–19, 28–38, 65, 102–121
See also banking-insurance conglomeration
economic aspects of financial conglomeration, 4, 7
legal aspects of financial conglomeration, 4, 7
financial development, 13, 48
financial firm, 29
financial group, 3, 34–36, 71–77, 105–115
See also financial conglomerate *and* banking-insurance conglomerate
cross-border formation of groups, 65
financial industry, 7, 95, 114
See also financial services industry, banking industry *and* insurance industry
financial institution, 1–2, 9–24, 35–38, 67, 82, 95, 106–121
financial instrument, 7–8, 12, 14
financial intermediary, 14, 71
financial intermediation, 11, 71
financial market, 28, 67, 103, 106, 112
financial operation, 9
financial performance, 23
financial product, 22–25, 30, 107
financial sector, 10–15, 24, 33, 69–84, 96, 105–121
See also banking sector *and* insurance sector
financial sector balance sheet threshold, 10
financial segment, 21
financial services, 3–29, 38, 60, 82, 97–118
financial services firm, 10
financial services group, 5
financial services industry, 1, 12–14
financial services market, 30
financial services provider, 1, 24–97, 101

financial services provision, 13, 68, 110–111, 119
    integrated financial services, 23, 99
financial stability, 26, 112–113
financial system, 71–72, 110–113, 121
financial technology, 13
firewalls, 31, 103
focused firm, 7
focused institution, 23

globalisation, 1, 23–24, 28, 117

holding 10, 61
    bank holding company structure, 9, 10
    financial holding company, 8
    financial holding company structure, 9
    holding company model, 9
    holding company, 9, 15, 39, 57, 103
    holding structure, 9, 61
    strategic holding, 88
home-country rule, 113

industrial group, 10
insurance, 7–15, 20–21, 33–36, 53–61, 72, 82, 108
    insurance acquisition, 94
    insurance activity, 22–33, 53–60, 67, 79, 86, 118
    insurance business, 3–4, 45, 53–57, 72, 87, 94
    insurance company, 3, 12–24, 45, 53–65, 72–82, 94, 102–103, 114
    insurance firm, 3–4, 21, 33, 45, 53–90, 94–103, 118
    insurance group, 57, 82–83, 120
    insurance industry, 15, 61
        See also financial industry *and* financial services industry
    insurance market, 4, 53–58, 72, 79, 83–84, 102, 119
    insurance product, 21, 60, 67, 100
    insurance provider, 57, 83–84, 101, 119
    insurance sector, 8, 53–59, 69–72, 79–82, 90–94, 109, 119
        See also financial sector
    insurance undertaking, 2, 10, 35, 53–65, 72–84, 90–95, 109, 117–118
integration, 16, 29–30, 35, 67, 113
    economic integration, 13, 27
    financial integration, 28, 30, 110
    financial services integration, 7, 16
    integration of banking activities, 98
    operational integration, 29, 30
internal contagion effect, 32, 34, 118
internal market, 110
intra-sector transaction, 67

investment, 27, 30, 86, 102
    financial investment, 110
    foreign direct investment, 102, 110–111
    investment firm, 3
    investment management, 8
    investment operation, 17
    investment project, 23
    investment services, 8, 12
    strategic investment, 104, 110–111, 121

knock-on effect, 36

lending, 22
life insurance, 58, 72, 79
    life insurance activities, 15, 53, 57
    life insurance business, 59
    life insurance market, 59
    life insurance segment, 58
linkage, 2–4, 38, 53–89, 104, 110–121
    banking linkage, 53, 57
    conglomeration linkage, 2, 103, 107, 111
    financial conglomeration linkage, 4, 111
    insurance linkage, 41, 45, 49
    insurance-banking linkage, 57
    systemic linkage, 112

macro-economic parameter, 11, 90
market power, 16, 20–23, 30, 38, 48, 117–118
merger, 14–20, 25–28, 31, 49, 71, 90, 107–109, 116–118
    bank merger, 2
    defensive merger, 17
    horizontal merger, 19
    insurance merger, 2
    merger motive, 4
    offensive merger, 17
mergers & acquisitions (M&A) activity 1–4, 13–30, 49–52, 65–84, 90–111, 118–120
    cross-border M&A activity, 13, 26–27, 65–67, 107, 118
    mergers & acquisitions (M&A) deal, 49, 90
    mergers & acquisitions (M&A) strategy, 96, 100–101, 120
    mergers & acquisitions (M&A) transaction, 60, 65, 118, 120
    mergers & acquisitions (M&A) trend, 94–95, 120
micro-economic parameter, 10–11
moral hazard, 34
multiple gearing, 32–33

new member state, 1–4, 69–90, 94–121

non-life insurance, 59, 72, 79
    non-life insurance activity, 53, 57
    non-life insurance business, 58, 59
    non-life insurance market, 59
    non-life insurance segment, 58

one-stop shopping, 19–20

parent-subsidiary model, 9
participating interest, 88, 90
participation, 8, 33
    banking participation, 76
    board participation, 14
    cross-participation, 15
profitability, 14, 103
    sales profitability, 60

rating, 106
regulatory arbitrage, 32, 39, 118
regulatory thresholds, 3, 67
revenue, 16, 22, 28
    revenue benefit, 105, 121
    revenue diversification, 16
    revenue effect, 29–30
    revenue efficiency, 19, 21, 106, 117
    revenue enhancement, 23, 105
    revenue stream, 30
    revenue synergy, 19
risk, 12–16, 22, 31–37, 101–103, 118
    credit risk, 12
    economic risk, 34
    insurance-related risk, 58
    market risk, 12
    reputation risk, 108, 121
    risk control, 98
    risk exposure, 34
    risk management structure, 109–110, 121
    risk management technology, 18
    risk management, 18, 21, 25, 30, 34–37, 106, 109
    risk of insolvency, 105
    risk of internal contagion, 34–35, 103
    risk-return performance, 16
    risk-shifting, 34
    standalone risk, 35
    systemic risk, 37, 58, 112–113, 121

safeguard, 16, 31–37, 118
securities, 12, 22
   securities activity, 14–15
   securities firm, 114
   securities house, 3
   trading in securities, 36
single market, 12–15, 114
single passport, 13
small and medium-sized enterprises (SME), 96, 121
   small and medium-sized enterprises (SME) lending, 115, 121
specialised firm, 16, 30–31
strategic alliance, 15, 52
subsidiary, 8–14, 32–39, 45, 53, 76–77, 82, 90, 103–114, 120
   operating subsidiary, 9
   regulated subsidiary, 33
supervision, 5, 27, 31–38, 111–118
   consolidated supervision, 31
   group supervision, 31
   solo supervision, 31
   supplementary supervision, 11, 31–34, 68, 117–119
supervisor, 31–37, 114, 121
supervisory arbitrage, 34, 114, 121
synergy, 9, 16, 29–31, 35, 104
   benefits of synergy, 67
   cost synergy, 18
   effects of synergy, 98
   industrial synergy, 7
systemic stability, 37–78, 110–113

too big to fail, 37, 112, 121
transparency, 11, 36–37
   lack of transparency, 32, 36–37, 118

veil piercing, 9